THORSONS
VEGETARIAN MICROWAVE COOKBOOK

Appetizing, imaginative recipes that make the most of your microwave.

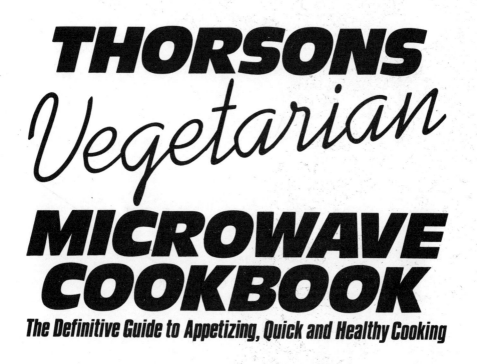

THORSONS
Vegetarian
MICROWAVE COOKBOOK
The Definitive Guide to Appetizing, Quick and Healthy Cooking

Cecilia Norman

THORSONS PUBLISHING GROUP

First published March 1987

British Library Cataloguing in Publication Data

Norman, Cecilia
Thorsons vegetarian microwave cookbook.
1. Vegetarian cookery   2. Microwave cookery
I. Title
641.5'636   TX837

ISBN 0-7225-1345-3

Published by Thorsons Publishers Limited,
Wellingborough, Northamptonshire, NN8 2RQ, England

Printed in Great Britain by Richard Clay Limited,
Chichester, Sussex

3   5   7   9   11   13   12   10   8   6   4

CONTENTS

ACKNOWLEDGEMENTS

Penny Morris, Jacqui Lambert and Vicky Pollard were the Home Economists who tested the recipes in the book, adding suggestions to my own ideas for what I hope are interesting dishes. Jenny Pouncett typed the manuscript and checked that the ingredients were listed correctly and Dorothy Bizzell read it to make sure it makes sense. My husband Laurie helped me to put the book together and my daughter Dilys donated recipes from her own collection. My thanks to them all.

INTRODUCTION

I have been interested in microwave cookery ever since 1969 when I wrote my first book. There weren't any cook books around for me to pick up ideas from, so I tried converting ordinary conventional recipes. It wasn't long before I discovered that microwaves cook differently and so I had to more or less forget adaptations and devise new and suitable recipes for use in the microwave only. I believe that microwaving is one of the best forms of cooking. At the same time, I fully accept that there are things that it cannot do, and then I use the conventional oven and grill as well.

I haven't always been a vegetarian and so I am fully aware that a meat eater's taste buds are different. Born vegetarians who have never tasted meat or fish flavours will not miss them, but the vegetarian convert may notice their lack, particularly of the glutinous textures of sauces and gravies.

Taking everyone's views into account, I set about producing dishes that could appeal to both these categories and also as many as possible which could be adapted for vegans.

Although many vegetarians may not be whole-fooders because they are willing to eat white rice and flour and sugar, we are advised that it is nutritionally healthier to use untreated and unrefined foods and so I have borne this in mind when compiling the recipes.

I have enjoyed all the recipes, as have my husband and friends, few of whom are vegetarians. All, however, are aware that a better diet includes less meat. I hope you like the recipes too.

THE VEGETARIAN AND MICROWAVE COOKERY

VEGETARIAN VARIETY

To be well-balanced and really appetizing, vegetarian food must be varied. Foods of different categories should be eaten at the same meal in order to make the best use of vitamins. Choosing basic foods of different colours also helps to ensure a balance, because they contain different nutrients.

Some vegetarians eat butter, some eat polyunsaturated margarine. Vegans do not eat butter or the polyunsaturated margarines which contain whey. Similarly many of the recipes call for milk, which can be whole or skimmed milk, or plant milk for vegans. In savoury dishes, you can use vegetable stock. Unfortunately it is not always possible to find substitutes for eggs, but vegetarian cheese is readily available. Bear in mind that substitutes will affect the flavours and textures of the dish. For example, sauces made with white flour are much smoother than those made with wholemeal flour, and a sauce made with vegetable fat, plant milk and wholemeal flour will taste quite different from the butter, white flour and whole milk variety. This is not to say that the results will be inferior—just different.

All vegetable oils are suitable for vegetarian cooking, but coconut oil is saturated and olive oil is mono-saturated. Corn oil and soya oil are polyunsaturated. Sunflower oil has the least taste, is the least viscose and is very high in polyunsaturated fats. Oil should be fresh, so don't store it for a long time, and don't continuously re-use oil that has been used for frying.

The move to a vegetarian diet should be a liberation from the restrictions of a 'meat and two veg' approach to dining. But it is important not to fall into the trap of serving a meal made up of similar colours, similar flavours, similar consistencies. That would be equally boring.

Because I feel strongly about this and also because I have my ever-ready microwave by my side, I am able to cook whenever I feel the urge and have time to spare and then freeze the results of my labours in small portions. The freezer, however small, goes hand in hand with the microwave, making eating more economical. When I am preparing a meal, all I have to do is to take a selection of cooked foods from the freezer, thaw and reheat them in the microwave and offer a selection of three or more different types of food. Fresh vegetables and salads don't take long to prepare. Frozen vegetables thaw and cook quickly in the microwave, so a full and varied meal can be on the table in minutes.

HOW THE BOOK IS SET OUT

You will see that the book is set out in three

parts. The next two chapters tell you about microwave cookery, including instructions for cooking all the basic foods; the middle section consists of new recipes for soups and main courses, desserts and jams; and the last Chapter contains menu suggestions, which may be of particular help to the new vegetarian.

DEFINITIONS

1. All spoons are British Standard measures. The 15ml spoon is equivalent to a tablespoon, and 5ml spoon is equivalent to a teaspoon. However, ordinary spoons will do as well in most recipes, but remember that spoon measurements must be level. To make sure of this, draw a tableknife across the rim of the filled spoon.

2. Unless otherwise stated, cook all dishes uncovered.

3. Suitable means that bowls, jugs and casseroles are microwave-proof.

4. A very large bowl has a capacity of 5 pints (2.8 litres); a large bowl, 3½ pints (2 litres); a medium bowl, 2 pints (1.1 litres); a small bowl, 1 to 1½ pints (570-850ml); and a small basin, under 1 pint (570ml).

The estimated servings are indicated at the top of each recipe but of course appetites vary and a smaller amount of each will suffice if other dishes are being included.

COOKING SETTINGS

Full Power means the maximum or highest setting on the domestic microwave of 600, 650 or 700 watts. Where 500 watts is the highest rating, add 20-30 per cent extra cooking time.

Defrost/Low is between 30 per cent and 38 per cent of Full Power. Markings on microwave ovens vary, so Defrost is sometimes shown as No. 3 or 4, and at other times as 30% or 40%.

If your machine has two or three settings below Defrost, use one mark lower to be on the safe side. 10% or Warm can be used for defrosting when time is not limited and when completely even results are required. Use this setting for keeping food warm, for helping to prove yeast doughs, or for defrosting egg custards and cheese dishes.

FREEZABILITY

At the end of each recipe there is a note about its freezability, and also whether the dish is suitable for vegans or can be adapted for vegans.

MICROWAVE MASTER CLASS

COOKING MICROWAVE

Microwaves cannot brown foods, cannot produce crusty exteriors with soft insides and must not be used for frying. You can buy combination ovens, which are conventional ovens with a microwave in one cabinet, and these often incorporate a grill. However, you can always use your traditional oven and grill to foods after cooking them in the microwave.

Some foods, such as sugar and syrup, do darken in the microwave, however. Nuts begin to burn quite quickly and dark ingredients, such as chocolate, carob, molasses or dark sugars, help to produce deep colours. Cooking results may look different from conventionally cooked food but they will be as good and often even better.

The microwave lends itself well to vegetarian cookery. Vegetables are particularly appetizing because they keep their colour and the just tender texture which vegetarians have always appreciated is how vegetables should be cooked.

HOW MICROWAVES WORK

It is worth spending time really getting to grips with microwaving, and there are certain techniques you should master. Microwaves heat by causing the molecules in the food to rub against each other. The faster the microwaves and the longer they are left to act, the greater the temperature in the food. When the required level of heat is reached and the electricity is switched off, the microwaves leave the food.

As far as microwaves are concerned, defrosting, reheating and cooking, are one and the same process. There is no special mystique about it. It's just a matter of the time needed to reach the correct temperature.

POWER LEVELS

Most ovens are calibrated from 1 to 10 or from Low to High, or have a number of settings at specific power levels. All models now have at least Full Power and Defrost settings. Thawing, reheating and cooking can be carried out on any setting, but for best results select the right one for the job. On most models the power remains constant at Full Power and on the lower settings there are inbuilt switch-off periods at regular intervals. During these rest periods the heat evens itself out throughout the food.

COVERING

When food is covered, heat cannot escape and so defrosting and reheating are speeded up. On the other hand, covered food loses its crispness, so you have to decide which is more important—speed or finish. It is definitely not a good idea to cover bread during defrosting, but casseroled food will thaw more quickly if the lid is left on.

Coverings can be kitchen or greaseproof paper, non-stick vegetable parchment, plastic film, plastic lids, casserole lids, or pottery or glass plates. Kitchen paper is absorbent, so it can be used underneath food to keep it crisp or as a covering to achieve the equivalent of steaming. Greaseproof paper and non-stick vegetable parchment can be used under the food instead of a plate, or for covering it when fast but not steamy cooking is wanted. Greaseproof paper may adhere to the food a little, but vegetable parchment will not. Plastic film is useful for covering the tops of dishes and bowls, but should not come into contact with hot food.

Plastic film must be vented to prevent it ballooning up, so remember to pull back a corner. Plastic lids usually have a built-in vent and will fit over most dishes. Ovenglass is wonderful because you can see through it, but plates cannot be vented so take care when removing them. Casserole lids usually have a lip or knob for easy removal and many are designed with a vent hole for steam to escape.

To Stir or not to Stir

Food that is stirrable—that is, for example, when stirring will not disturb the appearance —can be thawed and cooked on Full Power. It is essential to stir frequently, so that you don't follow a stone-cold spoonful with one that will burn your mouth. Always stir before serving, for the same reason. If you cannot stir the food, it must be reheated more slowly. Pies, quiches and layered dishes must be thawed on the Defrost/Low control, and some benefit from being cooked at this level.

Reheating

A plate of food, whether comprising a single or a mixed selection of items, can usually be reheated on Full Power. Leave uncovered those parts that you wish to remain crisp— for example, conventionally roasted potatoes. Sometimes one type of food will take longer to reheat, so put this on the outer edge of the dish because the microwaves attack the outer items more fiercely than those in the centre. Pasta, for example, is a slow defroster and reheater, so is best reheated either mixed in with the sauce, or arranged around the edge of the plate with the sauce in a well in the middle. Thin foods will reheat more quickly than thick ones, and slow-to-cook ingredients will be correspondingly slow to reheat. To reheat two plated meals, place one above the other, separated by a plastic stacking ring. Cover the top plate and do not arrange the plates so that two similar foods will be under one another. If, for example, you are reheating two plates of ratatouille, boiled potatoes and lentil cutlets, make sure that you don't have ratatouille above ratatouille, cutlets above cutlets, and potatoes above potatoes.

A meal on a plate takes about 2 minutes to reheat. Delicate foods such as quiches, egg custard and bread-and-butter pudding should be reheated on Defrost/Low as they will curdle and toughen if the microwave power is too high.

Timings

New microwave owners tend to expect the timings in cookery books to be exact. This cannot be so for many reasons:

1. The performance of the individual microwave will vary in the same way as similar cars have a different petrol consumption.

2. There can be a 10 per cent variant in the power output, which means that an oven marked 600 watts may be working at 660 watts or 540 watts, or any level in between.

3. Declared ratings vary from model to model. Recipe timings based on a 700 watt

correctly adjusted oven may not be much use if your own is rated at 600 watt and is on the slow side.

4. Line voltage of electricity coming into your house fluctuates, and you may find the same dish takes longer to cook at peak consumption hours.

5. The starting temperature of foods has an enormous effect and refrigerators vary in their 'coldness'. Cold food takes longer and, as I mentioned before, defrosting, reheating and cooking are one and the same process, so it's just a question of how long it takes to reach the temperature you require.

6. Old and stale ingredients may take longer than fresher or younger ones. Old runner beans are much tougher and need more cooking than young ones. Dry beans that have been stored for a long time also take longer to cook. The composition of food has an effect as well. Old potatoes boil more quickly than new potatoes, for example, because the sugar content has increased.

7. Speed of cooking is in direct ratio to the volume of the food. The more food you are cooking, the longer it takes.

8. A dirty oven interior is dangerous because the build-up of grease around the door seals will prevent the door from closing properly, and food particles stuck on the oven ceiling can cause arcing. Food spillage will increase cooking time considerably because the microwave cannot tell the difference between the dish you want to cook and the old spilt bits, so it will cook both.

9. The amount of liquid and its temperature at the start affect cooking times. Some foods, such as root vegetables, have to have a little more cooking water which diverts the microwaves away from the food itself.

All these factors will affect cooking times, so use the timings in the recipes as a guide only.

Food will cook more quickly if you start off with a well-heated bowl. You will notice this if you are using the same container for two consecutive processes.

CONTAINERS

Bowls, casseroles and dishes come in different shapes and sizes and microwave cookery must be carried out in the most suitable container. Food cooked in a tall-sided dish will take longer than food in a shallow dish. An oval dish hastens cooking because the microwaves cook more powerfully around the edges and the less activated area in the middle is narrower than in dishes of other shapes. If food is likely to boil up, use a tall container, otherwise use snug dishes that just fit around the food in them.

Micro-proof containers include Pyrex, Corningware, pottery, stoneware, plastics and plasticized paper. Although all have their place and value, some do slow down the cooking time. Cooking or roasting bags must not be sealed with metal tags but should be loosely secured with the plastic tab supplied, or by a rubber band. A ¾-inch (2cm) gap must be left in the top.

UTENSILS

Never use utensils with a metal content. They will cause sparking or, if they are thick, the food will remain cold because the microwaves cannot pass through the metal. Crystal, which has a lead content, will undoubtedly explode, and pottery or stoneware, which may have impurities in it, can become very hot. Only use containers made of materials which are resistant to the temperature of the cooked food—some plastics distort, for example.

Always protect your hands with oven gloves, just in case the dish is hot when you remove it from the oven. This may be nothing to do with the material the dish is made from, but can be caused by heat transference from the food. When removing covers, first lift the edge furthest from you so that escaping steam does not scald you.

BROWNING DISHES

Browning dishes are designed to sear and seal in a similar way to a frying pan. Specially designed for microwave, they have a tin oxide coating under the base. Some dishes have lids, but only the base is preheated in the microwave. First collect up an oven glove and a heat resistant board, put the dish in the empty microwave set on Full Power and switch on for the time recommended by the manufacturer. The base of the dish will become very hot. Add a knob of butter and use the browning dish with the lid for quick fried eggs, or without the lid for stir-fried vegetables, fried tofu and so on. Try to add ingredients without taking the dish from the microwave so that you don't lose heat. When you do remove the dish, stand it on the board, as although browning dishes are slightly raised, they get very hot and can damage or burn worktops.

ONE AT A TIME

Unless the manufacturers recommend differently, it is best to cook one dish at a time. Because foods are of different constituencies, and some are solid and dry whereas others are more watery, constant stirring and repositioning will take more time than it's worth if you try and mix the dishes in the microwave.

COOK BY LOOK

You should cook by look, just as you do with ordinary cookery, judging at each phase whether it is time to proceed to the next stage. My recipes have been prepared on a variety of microwaves and sometimes I even changed ovens halfway through. Nearly all the recipes give an indication of what should be happening at each stage and what the food therefore should look like at that point.

The Basic Repertoire

Heating Fats

So many recipes call for melted fat that this seems to me to be the first cooking process to learn. Put some butter or margarine into the bowl or casserole that you will be using to complete the dish. Do not cover. Melt small quantities on Full Power, and larger quantities on Defrost/Low. Stir as soon as the fat is half melted, then continue heating only if necessary. If the fat is left until fully melted, the outer area may splatter and start to clarify. Allow from 30 seconds on Full Power to 1½ minutes on Defrost/Low.

Heating Liquids

A large volume of water will boil quickest in the kettle. It is more economical to heat up to ½ pint (285ml) in the microwave.

Small quantities cook more quickly in the microwave, so it is better to use concentrated stock and dilute towards the end of the cooking. Milky fluids are always best heated in the microwave, because no sediment will stick to the bottom of the container, but do not use tall narrow bottles as the milk will shoot out at the top. Do not cover during heating. Baby's bottles must be warmed with extreme care and shaken vigorously to combine the hotter and cooler parts. Test by shaking a few drops on to your wrist before feeding to the baby.

Milk can be heated from cold to steaming point in the following times.

¼ pint (140ml)	1 to 1½ minutes
½ pint (285ml)	2¼ to 2½ minutes
1 pint (570ml)	3½ to 4½ minutes
1¾ pints (1 litre)	7 to 8 minutes

Milk for drinks is heated to a lower temperature of 60-65° (140-150°F) and this can be regulated if your microwave is fitted with a probe.

1 cup of milky drink takes 1½ minutes.

Soups are served at a slightly higher temperature because liquids cool more rapidly in a bowl and as the spoon is raised to the mouth.

1 bowl of soup takes 2½ to 3 minutes.

1 cup of black coffee takes 1½ to 2 minutes.

Water can be heated from cold to boiling point in the following times.

¼ pint (140ml)	1¾ to 2 minutes
⅓ pint (200ml)	1¾ to 2¼ minutes
½ pint (285ml)	2½ to 3 minutes
1 pint (570ml)	5½ to 6½ minutes

Unless you are making jam, liquids should be stirred during heating, particularly if they are being heated in bowls. This evens out the temperature, and also disperses air bubbles, which will otherwise grow larger and pop, causing many explosions.

FOODS IN SKINS

Any food sealed in by a skin or cover is likely to burst during microwaving. The longer it is in the microwave and the higher the power, the more likely this is to happen. There must be a place for steam to escape. Tomatoes will collapse. Apples need to be cored and scored around the waist with a sharp knife. Peppers must always be cored before cooking. Whole aubergines need only to have the stalk end removed. Oranges, grapefruit and lemons need piercing in one or two places. Eggs must not be cooked in their shells as they will explode, possibly with such force that the mechanism in the microwave is damaged; shelled eggs can be cooked without piercing under certain specified circumstances (see page 30). Whole fruit will not burst if it is first peeled. Plastic pouches of ready-to-thaw or ready-to-heat foods should be placed in a dish before slashing the top of the pack.

MICROWAVE TECHNIQUES

The basic microwave techniques are:

1. Stir during and once after cooking if food is stirrable.

2. Reposition the food, placing the pieces from around the outside in the centre.

3. Give dishes a quarter or half-turn during the cooking period. Areas where the microwaves bunch cook the food more quickly so that turning the dishes allows all the surfaces to pass under these hot spots.

4. Cover foods which benefit from a steamy atmosphere.

5. Pierce or score foods that will burst due to the build-up of steam and pressure inside them.

6. Shield with foil those parts of the food which cook more quickly than the rest. Use small smooth pieces of foil and cover them with greaseproof paper to prevent arcing.

7. Use the correct container which must be neither metal nor metallic-trimmed.

8. Don't run the microwave oven empty.

9. Keep the cabinet clean inside and outside. Use a soft cloth and washing-up liquid for cleaning.

10. Don't cook minute quantities on their own—for example, roasting ten peanuts.

11. Allow a standing time after cooking to enable less-cooked parts to catch up.

12. Don't overcook. More time can always be added.

13. Use the microwave in conjunction with your other appliances to increase your repertoire.

14. Use your own judgement for timings and cook by look and touch.

HERBS

The fresh flavour of newly gathered herbs cannot be surpassed. Dry the surplus in the microwave. Basil, sorrel, mint, tarragon, rosemary, chervil and parsley are just a few which can be used to perk up the vegetarian diet.

To dry herbs, rinse, drain and shake dry, then remove the leaves from the stems. Put a handful at a time between two sheets of kitchen paper in the microwave oven. Switch on at Full Power for 2 to 3 minutes, stirring the herbs frequently until they are just dry. Drying continues for a few more minutes during a short standing time. When cool, crush the leaves in the kitchen paper and put into jars or seal in small freezer bags.

Parsley sprigs should be watched carefully and stirred more often than the other varieties as the stalks tend to spark and burn during drying. To avoid this, cut as much of the stalk off as possible.

STEWED FRESH FRUIT

Apples, rhubarb and pears need no added water provided the dish is covered. Fruit does tend to boil up, however, so a deep container is recommended. Cook prepared fruit covered with vented plastic film or a vented lid and sweeten towards the end of cooking. 2 lb (900g) fruit will take 6-8 minutes and it is less likely to boil over if it is stirred occasionally.

Loganberries, boysenberries, raspberries and blackberries are usually eaten raw. To defrost only, put into a covered dish and stir occasionally using the Defrost/Low setting and allow about 6 minutes per lb (455g).

To cook fresh or frozen gooseberries, put the fruit in a deep dish, three-quarters cover and cook on Full Power, allowing about 8 minutes per lb (455g). Pierce the berries with a sharp knife as soon as they are thawed.

Blackcurrants, blueberries, redcurrants and cranberries are thawed by putting the fruit into a covered dish and heating on the Defrost/Low setting, stirring occasionally. Allow about 6 minutes per lb (455g). To cook, add 2-3 tablespoons water. Cover and vent, and allow 4 minutes per lb (455g) on Full Power.

Plums, damsons and greengages should be cooked in a deep dish with 3-4 tablespoons of water to each lb (455g) fruit. Cover and cook on Full Power, allowing 7-9 minutes per lb (455g). Add sweetening about halfway through.

The time saved baking apples in the microwave is enormous. Each apple only takes about 2 minutes. Sometimes they are highly successful and remain whole *but* at others they collapse and you find stewed apple oozing from the skins. Baked apple skins are usually tough when cooked in the microwave.

Make sure that the fruit is deeply scored with a sharp knife and that a ¾-inch (2cm) cavity is made all the way through the fruit when removing the core. Press any chosen filling into the cavity and turn the apples over halfway through cooking. When the apple is soft enough to squeeze, cover and leave to stand for 3-4 minutes.

DRIED FRUIT

With the exception of whole figs, there is really no need to soak dried fruit before microwave cooking. Put the fruit in a bowl or casserole and cover with cold water to reach about 1-1½ inches (2½-4cm) above the fruit. Cover, and vent if using plastic film. If using a non-vented lid, place a wooden cocktail stick between the lid and the dish so that the steam can escape. Cook on Full Power, shaking or stirring occasionally, until the fruit softens. Leave to stand for 10-15 minutes before uncovering. If too much liquor remains when the fruit is tender, remove the fruit and reduce the liquor by cooking uncovered on Full Power. Any pieces of fruit that protrude above the liquid may burn. Sweeten with raw cane sugar or honey towards the end of the cooking time. Reduce the timings on partly plumped (partially soaked) fruit.

Apricots, pears and peaches: Allow about 1 pint (570ml) water to 8 oz (225g) fruit.

Prunes and quartered figs: Allow about ¾ pint (425ml) water to 12 oz (340g) fruit. Cook covered for 10-15 minutes, stirring regularly or until the fruit is tender. Leave to stand for 10-15 minutes before serving.

To cook whole figs, cover with water and soak for 2 hours, then continue cooking as with other dried fruits.

To plump raisins and sultanas for fruit cakes, put the fruit in a bowl. Add fruit juice or water to barely cover. Heat, covered, on Full Power for 5 minutes. Leave to stand for 5 minutes before using.

VEGETABLES

All the wonderful reports that you have heard about vegetables cooked in the microwave oven are true. They retain their true bright colours, maintain an excellent texture and, because they are cooked in the minimum of water, precious vitamins are more likely to be saved.

Retain all the liquid from cooked vegetables to use as stock or to augment your other supplies of stock.

To make concentrated vegetable stock, peel and dice:

2 medium onions
1 large potato
1 large carrot
2 celery stalks

Place in a very large bowl with ¾ pint (425ml) water and 1 teaspoon vegetable oil. Cover and cook on Full Power for 10 minutes. Roughly crush the vegetables with a potato masher, then add a few sprigs of parsley, two bay leaves and sea salt and pepper to taste. Add another ½ pint (285ml) water, cover and cook for a further 20-30 minutes. Crush the vegetables once more, then strain through muslin and use as required. Use the cooked vegetables in soups or stews. The stock will freeze. As it is concentrated, freeze it in ice cube trays, so that you can use a single cube when you need to. This recipe is suitable for vegans and makes ½ pint (285ml).

Vegetables with a high water content need no added water, but most vegetables do appreciate a little water in the cooking. Vegetables are nearly always cooked on Full Power. If you are using salt, it must be added to the water and never sprinkled on to the vegetables before cooking. When vegetables are cooked without water, season after cooking.

To blanch vegetables, allow 4-5 tablespoons water to every lb (455g) prepared vegetables which should be cut into even-sized pieces. Combine in a covered bowl or casserole and cook on Full Power for 2 minutes. Stir to distribute the heat, then continue cooking for 1-2 minutes or until each vegetable piece is heated through. Drain once and plunge the vegetables into ice cold water, changing the water as soon as it warms. When the vegetables are completely cold, drain thoroughly and package for the freezer.

Frozen vegetables are cooked on Full Power.

Peas Cut beans Mange tout Carrots Cauliflower Sweetcorn Cabbage Broccoli Sprouts	Allow 8 tablespoons water to each 8 oz (225g) vegetables. If wished, mix ½ teaspoon sea salt into the water before adding the vegetables. Cook, covered, in a bowl or casserole for 5-7 minutes, stirring once during cooking although this does not make a great deal of difference. Leave to stand, covered, for 3 minutes before draining.
Corn on the cob	Put into a dish in a single layer, dab with butter or margarine. Cover with greaseproof paper. Cook on Full Power, turning over the cobs once during cooking. Cooking times: 1 cob: 4-6 minutes 2 cobs: 6-8 minutes 3 cobs: 10-12 minutes

To reheat canned or fresh vegetables, put the drained vegetables in a suitable serving dish, cover and heat on Full Power, allowing 1-1½ minutes per serving. Stir once during and once after cooking. If using a probe, set the temperature for 160°F (70°C).

COOKING FRESH VEGETABLES

Don't hope to cook 2 lb cabbage, 1½ lb runner beans and 2 lb potatoes and a sauce to go with them all in the microwave in less than an hour, unless you are blessed with at least two microwave ovens. Each vegetable will have to be cooked separately and at the end of it all, those you cooked first will have to be reheated. You can cook at least one of the vegetables in a pan on the hob and thus halve the cooking time of all the vegetables, or cook the vegetables one by one in the microwave earlier in the day and then reheat them, covered, just before serving. Whenever vegetables are to be reheated, undercook to start with.

The heavier the food, the longer it takes, as I have already said. I use the microwave to cook up to 1 lb (455g) of vegetables at a time. All the following instructions are for this quantity. Allow just over half the time for half the weight. Because vegetables are such an important part of the vegetarian and vegan diet, I have gone into quite a bit of detail about methods of preparing them.

The high water content vegetables need no added water. Among these are spinach, courgettes and marrow.

To cook spinach:

1. Wash the spinach and remove the tough stems.

2. Drain the leaves but do *not* shake off all the water.

3. Put the leaves in a casserole, bowl or roasting bag. If you are cooking them in a bowl, cover with plastic film and vent; cover a casserole with its lid; seal a roaster bag loosely with an elastic band or plastic (not metal) tab, leaving a finger-sized hole in the top for steam to escape.

4. Cook on Full Power for 5 minutes until the leaves collapse.

To cook carrots:
See pages 55 (whole) and 56 (sliced).

To cook courgettes:

1. Rinse, and top and tail the courgettes. Leave whole if they are small, otherwise slice or cut into sticks or chunks.

2. Put the courgettes in an oval dish or casserole, arranging them in a double layer. Sprinkle with nutmeg if liked, then cover and cook on Full Power for 5 minutes. Leave to stand, covered, for 4-5 minutes to soften the vegetables further.

3. Season to taste with salt and pepper.

To cook vegetable marrow:

1. Rinse and peel the marrow. A small marrow (1½lb/675g) can be cooked whole but it may turn out softer in parts. Otherwise, halve the vegetable lengthwise or cut into ¾-inch (2cm) slices. I like the pips and pith and can see no good reason to discard them, but that is up to you, of course. Put the marrow/squash into a dish—slices can be arranged in a double layer—and add a few dabs of butter. Cover and cook on Full Power for 8-10 minutes, repositioning the slices as they become translucent.

To cook tomatoes:
These need care.

1. Cut them in half and spread them out in a dish.

2. Season with salt and pepper and dab with butter if wished.

3. Cook uncovered on the Defrost/Low setting unless a large number of thick-walled tomatoes (beef tomatoes) are being cooked together. Remove each tomato as it is cooked. Four tomato halves will take about 2½-5 minutes. Salt is not usually used for cooking vegetables without water because it can dry them out, but tomatoes have so much natural moisture that this absorbs the salt without drying out the tomatoes.

To cook leeks:
Although a reasonably watery vegetable, leeks must be cooked in water to prevent them from becoming squeaky.

To cook whole, put the trimmed and washed leeks, preferably in a single layer, in a shallow dish. Add hot salted water to reach halfway up the leeks. Cover and cook on Full Power for 8-12 minutes, turning the leeks over and repositioning them halfway through cooking. Leave to stand for 5 minutes before uncovering. Save the liquor for use in stock as leeks give such a good flavour.

To cook sliced leeks after preparing and rinsing them, put in a casserole, adding ¼ pint (140ml) salted water. Season with milled black pepper. Cover and cook on Full Power for 6-8 minutes or until tender. Leave to stand for 3 minutes before serving. Reserve the liquid after draining for use in stocks or sauces.

To cook celery:

Celery retains its crunchiness when microwaved. Separate the stalks and trim if necessary, then cook whole or sliced. Put the celery into a casserole, add 5 to 6 tablespoons salted water, then cover and cook on Full Power for 10-12 minutes, stirring occasionally until the celery is tender.

To achieve a softer result, put the celery with ½ oz (15g) polyunsaturated margarine in a covered casserole. Cook on Full Power for 4-5 minutes, stirring or repositioning the celery twice during this time. Add 5-6 tablespoons hot salted water and continue cooking for 5-6 minutes.

Because of its flavour, the cooking liquid should be retained for use in stock.

To cook cabbage:

Cabbage needs only 8 tablespoons of salted water, but it must be stirred and turned during cooking or you will find a few browned and tough pieces among the otherwise beautifully cooked vegetable. Cut the cabbage into wedges or shred coarsely. It is surprising how much space cabbage takes up, so use a large bowl or casserole. Put in the cabbage and pour the salted water over it. Cover tightly and cook on Full Power for 9-12 minutes, stirring or rearranging at least once, but preferably twice, during cooking.

To cook corn on the cob:

Cut off the thick stalk. Leave the leafy husks but pull out the silk, then put the cobs in a dish or wrap up individually in greaseproof paper parcels. Cook on Full Power for 3-4 minutes per 12 oz (340g) cob, testing towards the end of cooking. If, after cooking for the suggested time, the kernels are still not ready, cover tightly and leave to stand for 5 minutes. The kernels wrinkle when overcooked.

To cook mushrooms:

Mushrooms need a little water and must be cooked covered, otherwise they dry out. Add 2 or 3 tablespoons but do not salt. Allow about 4 minutes per lb (455g). Mushrooms can be cooked whole, quartered or sliced.

To cook peas:

Peas from the pod taste quite different from their frozen relations. Remember that you will have to buy 2 lb peas in their shells to yield 1 lb. Put the shelled peas in a casserole or bowl with ¼-½ pint (140-285ml) salted water. Cover and cook for 10-12 minutes, stirring once.

To cook fennel:

Fennel has a lovely aniseed flavour and tastes fantastic in salads. Cook it by all means but only until it is crisp tender. Quarter or slice it, or cook baby fennel whole. Put it in a covered casserole, adding 4 tablespoons salted water, and cook on Full Power for 10-12 minutes, stirring or repositioning once during cooking.

To cook onions:

Cook whole, quartered, sliced or diced. Put onions into a casserole and add 4 tablespoons salted water. Cover and cook on Full Power for 10-12 minutes, stirring once during cooking. Turn large whole onions over halfway through cooking.

Cook chopped onions or shallots or onion rings in a covered casserole with 1 or 2 tablespoons vegetable oil if you are going to use them in other recipes. Sauté them uncovered to achieve a degree of browning. Stir frequently during cooking. Puréed onions can be stored in the fridge for a week or two and in the freezer indefinitely. Sauté uncovered until lightly brown, then purée in the liquidizer. Add a teaspoon of the purée to savoury dishes.

To cook okra:

Okra is also known as bhindi, Lady's fingers or gumbo. Rinse, top and tail and put into a covered casserole, adding 8-10 tablespoons salted water. Cook on Full Power for 5-7 minutes, stirring once. Leave to stand, covered, for 5 minutes before draining.

To cook potatoes:
Cook potatoes in their jackets to eat either as jacket potatoes or when you need speedy mashed potato. As no extra liquid is used in cooking, add a little milk when creaming them.

Scrub, rinse and dry the potatoes, then prick the skins thoroughly in the usual way. Put the potatoes on a piece of kitchen paper and cook uncovered on Full Power, turning the potatoes over halfway through cooking. Allow about 4 minutes for one 6-7 oz (170-200g) potato and 6-8 minutes for two potatoes. Four potatoes of this size will take about 15 minutes. Take away the kitchen paper immediately or it will stick to the potato skins. Do not overcook or the potatoes will be dried up and spongy inside. Potatoes can be kept hot for about half an hour if you wrap them in a clean thick towel.

To mash potatoes, scoop out the cooked pulp and mash with butter or margarine and milk, or with vegetable stock.

To boil potatoes, scrape and cut the potatoes into even-sized pieces and put into a roasting bag or casserole. When cooking in a roasting bag add a cupful of salted water. Seal the bag loosely with the plastic tab or an elastic band, leaving a hole for steam to escape. Place upright on a dish for safety. Cook on Full Power for 10-12 minutes, gently repositioning the potatoes halfway through cooking by pushing the outside of the bag with an oven glove.

To cook potatoes in a casserole, put them in the dish and add salted water to barely cover. Put the lid on the dish and cook on Full Power for 10-12 minutes, stirring the potatoes twice during cooking. Leave to stand for 5 minutes before draining.

Do not scrape or peel new potatoes—just rinse off the soil under the cold tap and wipe with kitchen paper. Cook in the same way as old potatoes.

Sweet potatoes should be cooked as for ordinary potatoes.

To cook asparagus:
Thin asparagus or sprue will cook in half the time it takes to cook the thick-stalked variety. 1½ lb (680g) bought weight will take 11-12 minutes. Bend the stalks and rinse carefully without damaging the tips. Break off the inedible end at the point where the stalk curves. Scrape the asparagus with a potato peeler. Arrange the spears in a rectangular dish so that they are in two layers, each pointing in the opposite direction. Add 6-8 tablespoons water, cover tightly and cook on Full Power for 3 minutes. Reposition the spears in a side-to-middle fashion. Recover and cook until the tips are tender but not soft. Leave to stand for 5 minutes before uncovering.

To cook swedes, celeriac and kohlrabi:
If you wish, you can peel the vegetables, then cube and cook as for parsnips. An easier way is to cook these craggy vegetables whole. After washing, remove a slice from the base and put the whole vegetable into a medium bowl. Half-fill the bowl with hot water, then cover with a plate and cook on Full Power for 10-15 minutes, turning the vegetable over halfway through cooking. Leave to stand for 5 minutes before uncovering, then insert a sharp knife into the vegetable through the base—the knife should reach the middle without too much pressure. Remove the vegetable with a slotted spoon, put on a wooden board and remove the skin with a sharp knife and a fork. Slice, then chop up or purée in a liquidizer or blender. On rare occasions you may find the flesh too hard as you try to chop it, but don't despair—put the chopped mixture back into the bowl, add a few tablespoons of water, then cover and cook for a few minutes on Full Power. Purée with the cooking water. Season after cooking.

To cook cauliflower and broccoli:
Cooking cauliflower and broccoli needs practice. It is risky to cook a whole cauliflower

23

in the microwave as the texture of the flower is so different from the texture of the stems. Cut the cauliflower into florets and slice the thick stem to use in salads or when making stock.

Broccoli is similar in its dual texture. Break into florets and slice the stem separately, but cook both parts together, placing the florets in the centre of a shallow dish and the stems around the edge. Add about 8 tablespoons salted water to the dish, then cover and cook on Full Power for about 8 minutes. Test, then continue cooking for 2 or 3 minutes. The vegetables become softer if left to stand, and you can complete the cooking in this way if necessary.

To be remotely successful, whole cauliflower must be cooked on Medium/50% or on Defrost/Low. Start with the stalk uppermost and turn over halfway through cooking. An average time for 1½ lb (680g) cauliflower is 15 minutes.

To cook beetroot:

I love to buy beetroots raw because they are such fun to cook. Just cut off the top stalks and leave the little tail in place. Rinse, then put 1, 2 or 3 vegetables at a time into a bowl, add hot water to reach halfway up the sides of the beetroot, then cook, covered, on Full Power for 10 minutes. Test for cooking with a sharp-pointed knife. Turn the beetroot over and cook for a few more minutes, then remove from the rosy liquid. Leave until cool enough to handle, then peel in the usual way.

To cook aubergine:

Aubergines require no salting when cooked in the microwave. The vegetable is seldom eaten on its own and is usually mixed with onions, tomatoes, nuts or cheese. Cook whole, having first detached the stalk and scored the sides with a sharp knife. Halve, then place in a single layer in a shallow dish with a few spoons of water. Cook, covered, on Full Power for 5-8 minutes. Sliced aubergine can be cooked without additional water, but must be covered tightly and stirred occasionally. Timings are similar for whole or halved aubergine. A delicious way to serve this vegetable is to cube and lightly microwave it, then mix with a batter made from Besan flour and water, lightly seasoned with sea salt and milled black pepper and spiced with ground cumin, cardamom and curry power. Deep-fry conventionally in fresh clean sunflower oil, then drain and serve hot.

To cook broad beans:

Broad beans must be detached from the pods before cooking by microwave. To 1 lb (455g) young broad beans, add 8 fl oz (225ml) water. Do not add salt. Cook in a covered bowl for 8-10 minutes, stirring two or three times during cooking.

To cook globe artichokes:

Wash thoroughly in cold water, remove the long thick stems and cut off the spiky leaf tips. Open out the leaves with the fingers and put the artichokes in a bowl containing a little salted water. Cover tightly and cook on Full Power until a leaf pulls easily away from the artichoke. A single artichoke needs no attention during cooking but when cooking more than one, put the vegetables in a large bowl, so that they can be repositioned during cooking. Leave to stand, covered, for 10 minutes before draining.

For one or two artichokes, add 8-10 tablespoons water and season with ½ teaspoon sea salt. For four artichokes, use a scant ½ pint (285ml) water. Cooking time for one artichoke is about 5-6 minutes. Two artichokes will take about 8-10 minutes and four artichokes about 15 minutes.

To cook Jerusalem artichokes, salsify, parsnips, pumpkin and baby turnips:

Peel, remove the cores and seeds where applicable, and cut the flesh into even-sized pieces. Put into a bowl or casserole containing a generous ¼ pint (140ml) salted water and a squeeze of lemon juice plus ½ teaspoon vegetable oil. Cover and cook on Full Power, stirring once, until the vegetables are crisply tender. Leave covered for 5 minutes before draining. Test for cooking after 10 minutes as young vegetables will cook more quickly than older, tougher ones.

To cook mange tout:
Mange tout—also called sugar peas—require very little cooking. Top and tail the pods and pull away any strings you can. Put into a casserole and add 4 tablespoons water and a dab of butter. Cover and cook on Full Power for 5 minutes. Stir and leave for 3 minutes before serving.

To cook peppers:
Sliced or chopped peppers are cooked as part of a recipe. Whole peppers are usually stuffed but if you wish, you can blanch them first. Remove the core and seeds and put the peppers, upright, in a dish containing 2 tablespoons water. Cover and cook on Full Power for 2-3 minutes.

Pasta

Things are really improving on the pasta front. Dry pasta (pasta asciutta, as it is called in Italy) is now being produced from wholewheat and buckwheat in several different shapes.

All types of pasta can be cooked by microwave and the main point to note is that fresh pasta will require hardly any cooking. When cooking lasagne, lower one or two sheets into boiling water, then microwave until the water reboils before adding a further two sheets. Separate spaghetti strands during cooking.

To cook wholewheat dry pasta:
For 8 oz (225g) wholewheat pasta, use 1-1½ pints (570-850ml) boiling water. Add 1 teaspoon oil to any quantity of pasta, and 1 teaspoon sea salt or more if wished.
1. Put the pasta into a large bowl or casserole. Spaghetti strands may have to be broken in half.
2. Make sure that the water is fully boiling—it is quicker to boil the water in the kettle.
3. Pour the water over the pasta. Quickly stir in the oil and salt. Cover and cook on Full Power for 3-5 minutes or until the water comes back to the boil.
4. Remove the cover, stir, then cook for 4-5 minutes until the pasta can be cut with slight pressure.
5. Stir, then cover tightly and leave to stand for 5 minutes before draining.

To cook fresh pasta:
Use similar quantities of pasta, oil and salt as for dry pasta.
1. Put the pasta into a large bowl or casserole.
2. Add fast boiling water, oil and salt.
3. Cook without covering on Full Power for 2-3 minutes until the pasta is al dente. Stir once during cooking.
4. Cover with lid and leave to stand for 2-3 minutes or until the pasta is to your taste. Drain and serve at once.

If you intend to reheat the cooked pasta later, reduce the standing time and cool the pasta under cold running water. Shake off as much moisture as possible, then cover and refrigerate.

Cooked dry pasta can be frozen, but it is best to mix it with a sauce first. This is suitable for vegans.

Rice

Rice is universally popular and whenever you choose to cook it, do so by microwave. You won't save any time but you will save all the palava of starchy water boiling up and spilling over the stove. The grains will be separate and the texture just right. I have suggested three methods of cooking rice, but it is important to use the all-in-one method when cooking the nutritionally superior brown rice, so that you do not throw valuable nutrients out with the cooking water.

You can make risottos and pilaus by cooking the rice in a little butter or margarine before adding the other ingredients. Fried rice is really cooked rice tossed in butter and it is especially good.

Cooked rice freezes exceptionally well, and thaws and reheats perfectly. Freeze in the quantities you are going to serve, then simply unmould on to a plate or dish. Defrost and reheat on Full Power. It doesn't really matter whether or not the dish is covered. Cooked rice will keep in the refrigerator for a couple of days but after that it becomes sour. Never wrap rice in foil for storage or you will end up with speckled rice and tiny perforations in the foil. Freezer bags or boxes are more suitable.

To reheat rice from cold, sprinkle with a spoonful of water which will allow for evaporation and prevent the rice from drying out.

The quantity of rice that can be cooked in the microwave depends on the size of the bowl or casserole that will fit into your oven.

To cook long grain white rice without measuring:

1. Rinse or pick over the rice unless it is the easy-cook kind. Put it into a very large bowl and add a little salt. Three-quarters fill the bowl with boiling water.

2. Stir once and cook, uncovered, on Full Power until the water boils. Continue cooking until a grain of rice will break when pinched with the fingertips.

3. Turn the cooked rice into a colander and cool under cold running water. Make a few wells in the rice with a wooden spoon handle and leave to drain.

4. Reheat the quantity you need on Full Power for 2 or 3 minutes. 4 oz (115g) takes about 10 minutes to cook and 1 lb (455g) takes about 15 minutes.

To cook long grain white rice in measured quantities:

1. Add 1 oz (30g) rice to 5½ tablespoons hot water and ¼ teaspoon salt. Stir the rice, water and salt together in a casserole. Cover with the lid and stir once during cooking. At the end of the cooking time the rice should be tender and most of the water absorbed.

2. Quickly stir and replace the lid to keep in the heat.

3. Leave for 5 to 6 minutes before checking again. If at the end of this time the rice is cooked, drain away the surplus liquid; if the rice is undercooked yet dry, on the other hand, add a little more water and continue cooking, covered, for a few more minutes.

To cook brown rice:

1. Brown rice absorbs twice as much water as polished rice, so the proportions you need are 4 oz (115g) brown rice to 1 pint (570ml) hot water and ½ teaspoon salt (optional). Put the rice, salt (if used) and water in a casserole.

2. Cover with the lid and cook on Full Power for 20-25 minutes or until the rice is nearly cooked and has absorbed most of the water.

3. Stir quickly, replace the lid and leave to stand for at least 5 minutes. Test the rice—if all the liquid has disappeared and the rice is still undercooked, add a few tablespoons of water and continue cooking for a few more minutes. Increase the cooking time by a half if the quantity of rice is doubled.

DRIED BEANS, PEAS AND LENTILS

These are known as pulses or legumes and are cheap to buy but rich in protein. First wash the pulses thoroughly in several changes of cold water, then drain in a strainer or colander.

There are two ways of soaking pulses:

1. The cold soak. Put the pulses in a large bowl, fill up to the rim with cold water and leave for a minimum of 4 hours.

2. The hot soak. This is a shorter method

which needs ¾ pint (425ml) hot water to each 4 oz (115g) beans. Combine in a large bowl and heat, covered, on Full Power until boiling. This will take at least 3 minutes. Remove the cover and cook for a further 3 minutes, then cover and leave to soak for at least an hour.

After soaking, rinse the beans again in several changes of cold water.

Beans from the kidney bean family—that is, the long flat kind—cannot be cooked in the microwave as they must be fast-boiled for at least 10 minutes to remove the toxins. After this period of time they can be finished off in the microwave. The kidney bean family includes black-eye beans, red kidney beans, lima beans, butter beans and borlotti beans. Adzuki beans and chick peas do not require this initial fast boil.

To cook beans conventionally: (When a weight is given, it is the dry weight of the beans) Put the beans into a large saucepan, remembering that they treble in size when cooked. For every 8 oz (225g) dry beans, first soak, then add 1¼ pint (680ml) hot water and 1 tablespoon vegetable oil. Bring to the boil and fast-boil for 10 minutes. Reduce to simmer and cook for 1 or 2 hours, depending on the variety and freshness of the beans. Add salt during the last few minutes of the cooking time. Drain, rinse and drain again before use.

To cook beans in the microwave:
Transfer the beans after the initial 10-minute boiling. Rinse in cold water, drain and put into a very large bowl. To each 8 oz (225g) beans add 1¼ pints (680ml) hot water and 1 teaspoon vegetable oil. Cover the bowl with plastic film, leaving a 1-inch (2½cm) gap, and cook on Full Power for about 30 minutes. Leave to stand for 10 minutes before uncovering, then drain, rinse and drain again before use.

Beans also cook very quickly in the pressure cooker—they only take one-third of the conventional cooking time.

Chick peas cook well in the microwave and do not need the 10-minute fast boil. Soak them overnight in cold water, then rinse and drain. Put into a large bowl with three times the volume of boiling water. Add 1 teaspoon vegetable oil, cover the bowl with plastic film, leaving a 1-inch (2½cm) gap, and cook on Full Power for 20-30 minutes, stirring once during cooking. Add salt to taste and leave to stand for 10 minutes before rinsing.

Lentils and split peas are very successful when cooked in the microwave and do not need to be pre-soaked. Pre-soaking does reduce the cooking time, however, which is useful if the microwave is needed for other cooking.

To cook split red lentils by microwave:
Rinse the lentils and put into a very large bowl. To each 8 oz (225g) lentils add 1¾ pints (1 litre) hot water and ½ teaspoon vegetable oil. Half-cover the bowl with plastic film and cook on Full Power for 25-35 minutes. Add more water during cooking if the mixture becomes too dry. Salt after cooking. Soaked lentils will take about half this cooking time.

To cook split peas add a further ten minutes cooking time.

Canned or frozen beans should be drained and rinsed before adding to dishes.

GRAINS AND CEREALS

Recent vegetarian converts may not have used a great variety of grains before. A visit to the local health food shop shows you what is available, but you may not feel inclined to invest in a large packet of what looks like bird food until you have some idea how to make use of it. Don't be put off, however, go ahead and buy at least one packet. You can use your microwave for both soaking and cooking.

I have found that couscous, roast buckwheat, Bulgur cracked wheat and millet are the most versatile cereals. Couscous is available in various sizes—it is made from semolina and resembles tiny white beads. You need about ½ pint (285ml) hot water to 4 oz (115g) couscous grains.

1. Put the couscous in a large or very large bowl and stir in the water. Cover and cook on Full Power for 2 minutes until the grains swell and absorb the water.

2. Pour through a strainer and cool under running water, separating the grains with a fork.

3. Shake away the surplus moisture, then turn the couscous into a clean tea cloth and wring dry. Remove the dried couscous, scraping the surplus from the cloth and use as required.

Serve as Tabbouleh, a mid-Eastern salad, or in place of rice with vegetable casserole or ratatouille.

Buckwheat grains are large and are available plain or roasted. Roasted buckwheat is a lovely caramel brown colour and so makes a change from the usual creamy coloured cereal. To produce a soft mixture which could be shaped into rissoles or loaves, use 16 fl oz (455ml) plus 2 tablespoons hot water to every 4 oz (115g) roasted buckwheat.

Combine the water and buckwheat in a large bowl and, without covering, cook on Full Power for 10 minutes or until the grains are a uniform brown colour and the water is fully absorbed. Stir occasionally during cooking.

For more separate and firmer grains which are suitable for serving in place of rice or in salads, use 2 oz (55g) buckwheat to every 8 fl oz (225ml) hot water.

1. Put the buckwheat in a medium bowl or casserole and cook, uncovered, for 2 minutes to dry roast.

2. Stir the water into the hot buckwheat and cook on Full Power for 7 minutes until the grains are tender but not soft.

3. Add 2 tablespoons hot water, cover and leave to stand for 5 minutes until the water is absorbed.

Bulgur cracked wheat, also known as

Burghul, is partially cooked before packaging and is a most attractive golden colour. Although it can be used without further cooking it must first be soaked in water for 30 minutes. To fast-soak and cook in the microwave, use ¾ pint (425ml) hot water for every 4 oz (115g) Bulgur cracked wheat.

1. Put the Bulgur in a large bowl and pour in the water.

2. Cook on Full Power for 4 minutes, then add an extra 2 tablespoons hot water.

3. Cover and leave to stand for 5 minutes.

Millet is obtainable in flakes and also as tiny pale grains. When cooked, the grains swell and become a creamy colour. To cook millet grains, use 8 fl oz (225ml) *cold* water for every 2 oz (55g) millet grains.

1. Put the millet grains and water in a medium bowl and, without covering, cook until boiling (about 3 minutes).

2. The millet tends to boil right up to the rim of the bowl during cooking, so it is important to stir occasionally during the second stage. Cook for a further 10 or 11 minutes until the grains are tender and the water is fully absorbed.

Millet flakes can be used as a topping for pies or in place of oats—they are very tasty when roasted. Roast 8 oz (225g) at a time and store in an airtight jar. To roast, spread the millet flakes out on to greaseproof paper in the microwave oven. Cover with a second piece of paper and cook on Full Power for between 5 and 10 minutes, stirring frequently until the flakes begin to brown.

Rye flakes can be roasted in the same way.

You can also make porridge in your microwave. After cooking, porridge will keep for a day or two in the refrigerator and will thicken considerably during this time. Add extra milk or water when reheating and stir frequently to prevent boiling over.

For every 3 tablespoons porridge oats use 5 tablespoons milk and 5 tablespoons water (vegans should use all water). When serving add salt and sugar to taste.

1. Mix the oats and liquid in a large bowl

and, without covering, cook on Full Power until boiling (about 1½ minutes for one person).

2. Stir well. Reduce the setting to Defrost/Low and cook for 2 minutes for each portion.

3. Stir in sugar and salt before serving.

All the cooked grains freeze, defrost and reheat well.

CROÛTONS

Add croûtons to soup or serve with scrambled eggs. You will need 3 slices wholemeal bread and 3-4 tablespoons vegetable oil.

1. Cut away the crusts and dice the bread.

2. Put the oil in a shallow ovenglass dish and heat on Full Power for 1-2 minutes.

3. Stir in the diced bread and toss to coat with the oil.

4. Cook on Full Power for 3-5 minutes, tossing occasionally, until the croûtons crispen. In the first minute the cubes will soften and they then crispen rapidly. Be careful not to burn the croûtons.

5. Drain the croûtons on kitchen paper.

Croûtons freeze extremely well and can be reheated from frozen or from room temperature. They are suitable for vegans.

NUTS

Use the microwave for refreshing or roasting shelled nuts and for cooking unshelled chestnuts. In vegetarian cookery it is usual to leave the skins on and it would seem sensible to all cooks to do the same. Strictly speaking, peanuts are not nuts at all, but are classified as pulses. They should be cooked in the same way as nuts, however. Shelled walnuts can be very bitter when stale, so use the microwave to refresh them.

To refresh walnuts:

1. Put the nuts in a bowl and add cold water to cover. Place the bowl in the microwave and cook on Full Power for 2 or 3 minutes until boiling. Drain.

2. Replace the nuts in the bowl, cover with cold water and repeat the process twice.

3. Drain the walnuts in a strainer under cold running water and when they are cool, transfer the nuts to a clean dish. Cover with cold water and refrigerate for several hours or even a day.

4. Drain and use in salads.

To roast nuts:

1. Spread the shelled nuts on greaseproof paper or non-stick vegetable parchment in the microwave oven.

2. Cook on Full Power, stirring the nuts frequently, until crisp. From time to time, cut a nut open to test as browning begins inside. It is not safe to roast very small amounts. Timings are hard to predict, but start checking after 2 minutes.

Flaked almonds take about 3-4 minutes for 2 oz (55g). Whole shelled nuts take about 3-4 minutes for 2 oz (55g). Dessicated coconut takes 2-3 minutes for 2 oz (55g).

Nuts burn easily and continue browning even after they are removed from the microwave.

To shell chestnuts:

Make a deep cut along one side and place ten at a time in the microwave alongside a jug containing 1 inch (2½cm) water. Cook on Full Power, examining the nuts every 15 seconds.

To roast pumpkin or sunflower seeds:

Spread the seeds on a circle of non-stick vegetable parchment and cook on Full Power, stirring frequently. 1 oz (30g) will take about 3 minutes.

EGGS

To coddle:

Two-thirds fill a jug with hot water and bring

to the boil in the microwave. Remove the jug. Lower in the eggs. Cover the jug and leave to stand for 5 minutes.

To boil:

Wrap each egg individually and completely in smooth clean foil. Put the eggs into a jug or bowl. Cover with fast-boiling water and, without covering, cook on Full Power for 3-5 minutes for soft-boiled and 10-15 minutes for hard-boiled. It does not matter how many eggs are being cooked—the microwaves are heating the water and not the eggs. Remove the eggs with a slotted spoon, put them on to a cloth to absorb excess moisture, then unwrap carefully.

To poach:

Poach eggs individually in cereal bowls which are large enough to hold ¼ pint (140ml) water and narrow enough to prevent the egg white from spreading too far.

1. Stir a pinch of salt into the water in a cereal bowl and cook on Full Power for 2½ minutes or until boiling.

2. Immediately break the egg into the centre of the bowl. Cover with a saucer and cook on Full Power for 40-50 seconds.

3. Carefully remove the saucer and take out the egg with a slotted spoon.

Note: Use the same dish of water for cooking subsequent eggs.

To bake:

Use ramekin dishes or microwave poaching dishes.

1. Lightly oil the dishes and break an egg into each. Cover each dish with a circle of a suitable plastic film or non-stick vegetable parchment.

2. If cooking one egg, place it in the centre of the oven. When preparing more, arrange the dishes in a circle in the microwave.

3. Cook on Defrost/Low for about 2 minutes for one egg, 3 minutes for two eggs and 4 minutes for four eggs. Cooking times are a matter of personal preference. The eggs may not all cook at the same rate, so each egg should be removed as soon as it is ready. When the microwave has a metal turntable, cook egg dishes on the rack provided.

To scramble:

1. In a cup, jug or bowl, beat the eggs with 1 tablespoon milk or water for each egg. Season to taste with sea salt and freshly milled black pepper. Add a knob of butter or margarine if wished.

2. Cook on Full Power, beating with a fork every 30 seconds, until the eggs are loosely cooked. The mixture will continue setting for a few moments after the current is switched off.

Micro-fried eggs:

1. Preheat the empty browning dish in the microwave according to the manufacturer's directions.

2. Without removing the dish from the microwave, quickly add a teaspoon of oil or butter and break in the egg. Cover with a lid and cook on Full Power for 10 seconds only. Leave for a further 10 seconds before serving. To cook more than one egg, slightly increase the oil or butter and break one egg into each corner of the dish. Cook, covered, for 5 seconds per egg, removing each as it is ready.

PASTRY

Conventionally baked wholemeal pastry is usually rather solid and bread-like in texture. Microwaved wholemeal pastry is deliciously crisp and well worth making.

It is easier to microwave than pastry made with white flour. You can make it entirely with oil, but the colour will be darker and less attractive. The amount of water needed varies according to the flour used.

Imperial (Metric):
4 oz (115g) wholemeal flour
Pinch sea salt
½ teaspoon baking powder
1 tablespoon sesame seeds
2 oz (55g) polyunsaturated margarine
1 teaspoon vegetable oil
Approximately 3 tablespoons cold water

1. Mix the flour, salt, baking powder and sesame seeds in a bowl.

2. Add the margarine and oil and blend in with a fork.

3. Add sufficient water to form a soft dough. The amount varies according to the absorbency of the flour.

4. Knead the dough lightly and wrap in cling film. Chill for 30 minutes.

5. Roll out the dough to fit a 6½-inch (17cm) round pie dish and cook on Full Power for 3-4 minutes, giving the dish a quarter-turn three times during cooking. When the pastry is cooked it will have a dry appearance. When a filling is to be added, followed by further cooking, err on the safe side and initially cook the pastry for the minimum time.

BASIC WHITE SAUCE

Sauces form the basis of so many recipes and they are foolproof in the microwave. From the basic recipe you can produce an infinite number of sweet and savoury sauces and, of course, soups. Sauces made with wholemeal flour are slightly different from those made with white flour. While appreciating that most readers will prefer to use untreated flour, I am including a basic recipe for a sauce using unbleached white flour.

When making a white sauce with white flour, use the regular proportions. Use 1 pint (570ml) liquid to produce 1 pint of sauce.

Pouring sauce:
1 oz (30g) butter or margarine
1 pint (570ml) milk
1 oz (30g) white flour

Coating sauce:
2 oz (55g) butter or margarine
1 pint (570ml) milk
2 oz (55g) white flour

To make the sauce:

1. Put the butter or margarine in a medium bowl and heat on Full Power for 20 seconds or until nearly melted.

2. Stir in the flour with a wire whisk and cook for a further 20 seconds until the mixture is puffy.

3. Add the milk all at once and cook for 1½ minutes for ½ pint (285ml) or 2½ minutes for 1 pint (470ml).

4. Whisk thoroughly. Do not worry about the lumps, as they will soon disappear.

5. Continue cooking for a further 1½-2½ minutes, whisking every half minute until the sauce thickens.

WHOLEMEAL BASIC WHITE SAUCE

Makes 1 pint (570ml) pouring sauce

Imperial (Metric):
¾ oz (22g) butter or margarine
¾ oz (22g) wholemeal flour
1 pint (570ml) milk

1. Put the butter or margarine into a large bowl and heat on Full Power for 30 seconds until just melted.

2. Stir to complete the melting, then work in the flour. The mixture will not form a smooth paste. Cook for 20-30 seconds until the mixture is granular.

3. Add the milk all at once and use a wire whisk to mix. Cook on Full Power for 5 minutes, whisking frequently. The sauce will bubble and rise up and may seem undercooked even when this happens. Continue cooking for a further minute, then whisk again.

4. Season to taste and add any extra ingredients.

WHOLEMEAL BASIC SAUCE (USING OIL)

Makes 1 pint (570ml) pouring sauce.

Imperial (Metric):
1½ oz (45g) wholemeal flour
1½ tablespoons sunflower oil
1 pint (570ml) milk

1. Blend the oil and flour together in a large bowl and stir in the milk. The mixture will be full of small lumps.

2. Cook on Full Power for 4 minutes,

whisking occasionally. After this time the sauce will boil up and appear separated. Continue cooking for a further 2 or 3 minutes, whisking frequently, until the sauce thickens.

3. Season the sauce to taste and stir in additional flavouring ingredients.

A half quantity of sauce takes about half the cooking time.

Sauces will freeze, but must be liquidized and thinned down when reheating.

White sauces based on white flour may be sweetened with honey or raw cane granulated sugar and flavoured with carob, chocolate, vanilla or fruit purée.

Savoury suggestions include adding to taste any of the following: grated cheese; chopped hard boiled egg; chopped capers; chopped gherkins; grated lemon and orange zest; puréed cooked spinach; puréed cooked carrots; ground almonds; mustard powder.

Basic proportions for a pouring sauce:
For each pint (570ml) liquid use:

Imperial (Metric):
¾ oz (22g) wholemeal flour
¾ oz (22g) butter or margarine

Basic proportions for a coating sauce:
For each pint (570ml) liquid sauce:

Imperial (Metric):
1½ oz (45g) wholemeal flour
1½ oz (45g) butter or margarine

Wholemeal-based sauces thicken further on standing so add extra milk if necessary and reheat the sauce to cook in the added milk.

Sauces can also be made with oil instead of butter or margarine. These tend to be thicker and darker but can be made by the all-in-one method which eliminates one cooking step.

Basic proportions for an oil-based pouring sauce:
For each pint (570ml) liquid use ¾ oz (22g) wholemeal flour and 1 tablespoon sunflower oil.

Basic proportions for an oil-based coating sauce: For each pint (570ml) liquid use 1½ oz (45g) wholemeal flour and 1½ tablespoons sunflower oil.

VEGAN WHOLEMEAL SAUCES

Substitute vegetable stock for the milk and cook in the same way as the all-in-one wholemeal sauce. Use a large bowl and whisk the sauce frequently—sauces using stock boil up much more than milk-based sauces and need an extra minute or two to thicken. The colour of the sauce will be more creamy than white and will vary according to the colour of the stock.

Add tomato purée, yeast extract or a generous tablespoon of freshly chopped parsley or other fresh herbs during or after cooking. You can add puréed cooked carrots, celery, onions, leeks or mushrooms to make different accompaniments for nut roast, vegetables, grains or pasta.

SOUPS

Soups are very easy to cook in the microwave and a selection of methods is included in the recipes. However, if you want to make a quick soup using your own ideas, all you have to do is to make a thin white sauce. Cook to a purée your choice of vegetable, then mix the sauce and the vegetable together, adding seasonings and herbs to suit yourself.

Make soups in a very large bowl and double the quantity if you wish, adding a little extra time to that given in the recipes.

The maximum quantity that can be made at one time in the microwave is 4 pints (2¼ litres). If you make the soup very thick, an equivalent volume of stock can be added when reheating. An added bonus is that soups freeze so well.

Soups look very attractive when they are garnished. Add chopped parsley, a swirl of cream, julienne strips of cucumber, peppers, carrot or orange, or top with microwaved croûtons (see page 29) for special occasions.

Artichoke Soup

Makes 1½ pint (850ml)

Imperial (Metric):
4 large globe artichokes
1 egg yolk
4 tablespoons double cream
Sea salt
Freshly milled black pepper

1. Cut off and discard the long stem from the base of the artichokes and remove the tips of the leaves with scissors. Wash the artichokes thoroughly under cold water, opening the leaves slightly while doing so.

2. Put the artichokes in a large casserole dish with the bottom ends towards the outside. Add about ½ pint (285ml) water, cover and cook on Full Power for 15 minutes. Reposition the artichokes so that the top of each artichoke is immersed in the water. Re-cover and continue cooking for a further 10-15 minutes until a leaf can easily be pulled off.

3. Carefully remove the cover and take out the artichokes, leaving the cooking liquid in the bowl.

4. On a board, scrape the flesh from the leaves, remove and discard the hairy choke and dice the artichoke bottoms.

5. Measure the cooking liquid and make up to 1¾ pints (1 litre) with very hot water. Stir in the pulp from the leaves and the diced artichoke bottoms and cook on Full Power for 11-13 minutes until the liquid is slightly reduced. Purée the soup in the liquidizer or blender.

6. Beat the egg yolk and cream together. Stir in 2 or 3 tablespoons of the hot liquid, then strain into the soup. Season to taste with salt and pepper, then reheat on Full Power for 2-3 minutes, stirring once during and once at the end of cooking.

Note: The soup may be frozen up to the end of stage 4. Thicken with the egg yolk and cream during thawing and reheating. The sauce is *not* suitable for vegans.

Barley Soup

Makes 1¼ pints (710ml)

Imperial (Metric):
2 × 14 oz (395g) cans tomatoes
1 small young turnip, peeled and finely diced
3 tablespoons tomato purée
2 vegetable stock cubes
1 oz (30g) pearl barley
1 teaspoon dried basil
¼ teaspoon dried oregano
1 pint (570ml) water
Sea salt
Freshly milled black pepper

1. Purée the tomatoes in the liquidizer or blender and strain into a very large bowl. Discard the seeds.

2. Add all the remaining ingredients to the tomato liquid and mix well. Cover and cook on Full Power for 10 minutes or until fast boiling.

3. Carefully remove the cover and continue cooking the soup on Full Power for 30-35 minutes, stirring occasionally, until the barley is tender. Add salt and pepper to taste.

Note: The soup freezes well, improving the tenderness of the barley. It is suitable for vegans.

Beetroot Soup

Makes 2 pints (1.1 litres)

Imperial (Metric):
1 lb (450g) small raw beetroot
1 medium onion
**2¼ pints (1.3 litres) hot vegetable
stock**
1 oz (30g) Bulgur cracked wheat
2 tablespoons cider vinegar
¼ teaspoon bayleaf powder
¼ pint (140ml) milk
Sea salt
Freshly milled black pepper
1 small cucumber, finely diced
**2 tablespoons sour cream or 3
tablespoons natural low fat yogurt**

1. Peel the beetroot and the onion and
put into a very large bowl with the
stock, Bulgur, vinegar and the bayleaf
powder.

2. Cover the bowl with vented cling-film
and cook on Full Power for 18-20
minutes or until the beetroots are tender.

3. Drain into another bowl and remove
the beetroot and onion, leaving the
Bulgur in the strainer. Cut up the
beetroot and onion and purée in the
liquidizer with the milk.

4. Pour the purée into the hot liquid in
the bowl and stir in the Bulgur. Season
to taste with salt and pepper.

5. Add the diced cucumber to the soup,
then cover and cook on Full Power for 5
minutes or until boiling around the
edges.

6. Carefully uncover, stir the soup briskly
and finally mix in the cream or yogurt.

Note: Freeze at the end of stage 5, and
stir in the yogurt or cream after thawing
and reheating. Vegans should use
vegetable stock instead of milk and omit
the cream or yogurt.

Carrot Soup

Makes 1¾ pints (1 litre)

Imperial (Metric):
1 lb (455g) carrots
1 teaspoon sunflower oil
1 pint (570ml) water
1 × 14 oz (395g) can tomatoes
2 teaspoons dried chervil
¼ teaspoon bayleaf powder
Dash Holbrook's sauce
Sea salt
Freshly milled black pepper

1. Peel and finely slice the carrots. Mix
in a large bowl with the oil and 2
tablespoons of the water. Cover and
cook on Full Power for 5 minutes or
until the carrots are just tender. Do not
drain.

2. Stir the tomatoes, their juice, the
chervil, bayleaf powder and Holbrook's
sauce into the carrots and season to taste
with salt and pepper. Cover and cook on
Full Power for 4 minutes or until the
carrots are very soft.

3. Purée the mixture in the liquidizer or
blender, then return it to the bowl. Stir
in the remaining water, three-quarters
cover and cook on Full Power for 2
minutes or until the soup boils around
the edges. Stir thoroughly, then cook for
a further 2-3 minutes until the bubbles
reappear.

4. Stir before serving, adjusting seasoning
to taste.

Note: The soup freezes well—stir briskly
and frequently when thawing and
reheating. It is suitable for vegans.

GREEN LENTIL SOUP

Makes 1½ pints (850ml)

Imperial (Metric):
4 oz (115g) green lentils
1 small onion, peeled and finely
chopped
1 celery stalk, finely chopped
¾ oz (20g) butter or margarine
1¼ pint (710ml) hot vegetable stock
1 teaspoon yeast extract
¼ teaspoon bayleaf powder
¼ teaspoon turmeric
Sea salt
Freshly milled black pepper

1. Wash the lentils in plenty of cold water and drain thoroughly.

2. Put the lentils, onion, celery and butter into a very large bowl. Cover and cook on Full Power for 5 minutes, stirring occasionally.

3. Add the stock, yeast extract, bayleaf powder and turmeric. Cover and cook on Full Power for 5 minutes until boiling rapidly.

4. Uncover and cook for a further 25-30 minutes or until the lentils are soft, stirring occasionally during cooking.

5. Purée in the liquidizer or blender. Return to the bowl and add more stock if required. Season to taste with salt and pepper.

6. Cover the bowl and cook on Full Power for 5 minutes, stirring once during and once after cooking.

Note: This soup freezes well. It is suitable for vegans.

LEEK AND TOMATO SOUP

Makes 2½ pints (1½ litres)

Imperial (Metric):
2 large leeks, trimmed, washed and
finely sliced
1 pint (570ml) boiling water
1 pint (570ml) tomato juice
½ teaspoon dried basil or 2
teaspoons freshly snipped basil
6 tomatoes, sliced
½ teaspoon arrowroot
Sea salt
Freshly milled black pepper

1. Combine the leeks and ½ pint (285ml) of the water in a very large bowl, cover and cook on Full Power for 6 to 8 minutes, stirring occasionally until the leeks are tender. Purée in the liquidizer or blender.

2. Pour the leek purée back into the bowl and add the tomato juice and basil. Continue cooking for 3-5 minutes until hot, then stir in the remaining water and the sliced tomatoes. Cook on Full Power for 2-3 minutes until boiling around the edges.

3. Blend the arrowroot with a tablespoon of cold water, stir into the hot soup and cook on Full Power for 1-2 minutes. Season to taste with salt and pepper and serve hot.

Note: This soup improves upon standing but should not be kept in the refrigerator for more than one day. The soup freezes well. It is suitable for vegans.

LETTUCE SOUP

Makes 2 pints (1.1 litres)

Imperial (Metric):
**1 large cos lettuce, rinsed and
trimmed
½ oz (15g) butter or margarine
½ bunch spring onions, trimmed
and finely sliced
1 tablespoon finely chopped parsley
Pinch grated mace
2 tablespoons wholemeal plain flour
1 pint (570ml) hot vegetable stock
½ pint (280ml) milk
Sea salt
Freshly milled black pepper
2 tablespoons double cream**

1. Coarsely shred the lettuce. Put the butter or margarine into a large bowl with the spring onions. Cover and cook on Full Power for 3 minutes to soften the onions.

2. Mix in the parsley and mace with the lettuce. Cover and cook for 5 minutes until the lettuce is soft.

3. Blend the flour with 2 tablespoons cold water and stir into the lettuce mixture, then add half the hot stock. To thicken, cover and cook for a further 3 minutes.

4. Purée the soup in the liquidizer or blender, then pour back into the bowl. Stir in the milk and remaining stock. Reheat for 2-3 minutes on Full Power, stirring when the soup bubbles around the edges.

5. Season to taste with salt and pepper and stir in the cream just before serving.

Note: The soup freezes well. It is suitable for vegans if vegetable fat and vegetable milk are used and the cream is omitted.

MULLIGATAWNY SOUP

Makes 1¼ pints (700ml)

Imperial (Metric):
**2 medium potatoes, peeled and diced
2 medium carrots, scraped and
thinly sliced
½ small red pepper, thinly sliced
½ small green pepper, thinly sliced
1½ pints (850ml) hot water
½ pint (285ml) tomato juice
1 teaspoon curry powder
½ teaspoon cumin
½ teaspoon turmeric
½ teaspoon coriander
Sea salt
Freshly milled black pepper
2 tablespoons thick-set natural
yogurt**

1. Put the vegetables into a 2 pint (1.1 litre) bowl and add ½ pint (285ml) hot water. Cook covered on Full Power for 8 minutes or until the vegetables are tender.

2. Remove the vegetables with a slotted spoon and purée in the liquidizer or blender. Pour the purée back into the stock.

3. Add the tomato juice, the remaining water, the spices and the seasonings.

4. Cover and cook on Full Power for 3 minutes or until the soup is bubbling around the edges. Stir and heat for a further minute, then blend in the yogurt.

Note: This soup freezes adequately but it would be better to add the yogurt after thawing and reheating. Vegans should omit the yogurt.

MUSHROOM SOUP

Makes 1¾ pints (1 litre)

Imperial (Metric):
**12 oz (340g) button mushrooms
1 small onion, peeled and quartered
½ small clove garlic, peeled and
crushed
1½ pints (850ml) strong hot
vegetable stock
1 teaspoon soy sauce
Sea salt
Freshly milled black pepper
4 tablespoons single cream**

1. Slice and set aside 4-6 mushrooms. Roughly cut up the remainder and purée in the liquidizer or blender with the onion, garlic and 1 pint (570ml) of the stock.

2. Pour the mixture into a very large bowl, cover and cook on Full Power for 15-18 minutes, stirring occasionally.

3. Add the remaining stock and soy sauce, and season to taste with salt and pepper. Cover and continue cooking for a further 2-3 minutes or until boiling around the edges. Stir thoroughly.

4. Stir in the cream and float the raw mushroom slices on top.

Note: This can be frozen up to the end of stage 3, adding the cream and fresh ganish when thawing and reheating. It is a suitable dish for vegans if the cream is omitted.

VICHYSSOISE

Makes 2 pints (1.1 litres)

Imperial (Metric):
**1 large onion, peeled and finely
chopped
1 tablespoon vegetable oil
1 lb (455g) potatoes, peeled and
diced
12 oz (340g) leeks, trimmed, washed
and finely shredded
1½ pint (850ml) hot vegetable stock
Sea salt
Freshly milled black pepper
3 tablespoons natural yogurt
1 tablespoon freshly chopped parsley**

1. Put the onion and oil in a very large bowl. Cover and cook on Full Power for 3 minutes or until the onion is soft but not coloured.

2. Stir in the potatoes and leeks. Cover and cook on Full Power for 5 minutes.

3. Add half the stock. Cover and cook on Full Power for 15 minutes, stirring occasionally until the vegetables are soft.

4. Purée the soup in the liquidizer or blender, then return to the bowl and add the remaining stock. Season to taste with salt and pepper and leave to cool.

5. Chill the soup in the refrigerator and then stir in the yogurt. Sprinkle with parsley.

Note: Freeze the soup if wished but add yogurt after thawing. The soup can also be served hot by reheating before adding the yogurt. Vegans should omit the yogurt.

WATERCRESS SOUP

Makes 1½ pints (850ml)

Imperial (Metric):
2 bunches watercress
1 pint (570ml) vegetable stock
1 oz (30g) wholemeal flour
1 oz (30g) butter or margarine
½ pint (285ml) milk
Sea salt
Freshly milled black pepper

1. Rinse the watercress in cold water. Remove and discard the coarse stalks. Reserve a few leaves for garnish and put the remaining watercress into a large bowl with ½ pint (285ml) of the stock.

2. Cover and cook on Full Power for 3-6 minutes until the liquid boils, then cook for a further 8-10 minutes until the watercress is tender.

3. In a small bowl blend together the flour and butter. Add the paste in small dabs to the boiling mixture and beat vigorously to prevent small lumps forming.

4. Purée the soup in the liquidizer with the remaining ½ pint (285ml) stock. Pour back into the bowl.

5. Stir the milk into the smooth soup and cook on Full Power for 2 minutes or until bubbles appear around the edges. Stir, cook for a further 2-3 minutes and stir in the salt and pepper.

6. Garnish with the reserved watercress leaves.

Note: The soup freezes well. Vegans should substitute vegetable fat and vegetable milk.

SALADS

Salads do not require cooking but cooked ingredients are frequently used in them. Use the microwave to help increase your repertoire by cooking pasta, rice, buckwheat and vegetables, and browning nuts and seeds to mix with raw salad items.

Store salads in a cool place and use within a few hours so that they are really fresh.

Artichoke Salad

Serves 4 as a side dish.

Imperial (Metric):
**1 × 14 oz (400g) can artichoke
bottoms, drained and rinsed
2 tablespoons water
2 tablespoons sweet white wine
½ teaspoon fresh lemon juice
1 bay leaf
¼ teaspoon grated nutmeg
¼ teaspoon clear honey
Pinch sea salt
½ teaspoon vegetable oil**

1. Cut the artichoke bottoms into quarters and set aside.

2. Mix all the remaining ingredients together and cook on Full Power for 1½ minutes or until boiling.

3. Gently mix the artichokes into the marinade and heat until the liquor comes back to the boil (about 30 seconds).

4. Leave until cold before serving.

Note: Do not freeze but the marinade can be prepared several hours ahead. This is suitable for vegans—may substitute raw cane sugar for honey if wished.

Beetroot Salad

Serves 4

Imperial (Metric):
1 lb (455g) beetroots

Dressing:
**1 teaspoon clear honey
2 tablespoons vegetable oil
1 tablespoon raspberry vinegar
1 teaspoon freshly chopped parsley
Sea salt and freshly milled pepper to
taste**

1. Remove any long stalks and wash the beetroots, without damaging the skins.

2. Put the unpeeled beetroots into a large bowl with sufficient water to come halfway up the vegetables. Cover with vented cling-film. Cook on Full Power for 10 minutes until the beetroot is tender but not soft.

3. Using a slotted spoon, remove the beetroot from the water. Leave to cool for 10 minutes before peeling and dicing. Set aside.

4. Place the honey in a small basin. Cook on Full Power for 10 seconds to melt.

5. Stir in the oil and vinegar. Mix in the parsley and season to taste.

6. Pour the dressing over the diced beetroot. Mix well. Chill in the fridge for 20 minutes before serving.

Note: May be frozen but add extra fresh parsley after thawing at room temperature. This is suitable for vegans.

Cyprus Salad

Serves 4

Imperial (Metric):
**4 oz (115g) Haloumi cheese
Grated zest and juice of 1 lime
2 dessert apples
4 celery stalks, finely sliced
8 spring onions, finely sliced
Sea salt
Freshly milled black pepper
6 black olives, pitted and sliced
¼ pint (140ml) natural yogurt**

1. Dice the cheese, mix with the lime juice and zest. Stir well, cover and set aside for 30 minutes, stirring once.

2. Remove the cheese and set aside.

3. Core and dice the apples and mix into the marinade. Add the celery and onions, cover and cook on Full Power for 4 minutes to soften but not cook. Season with salt and pepper. Leave to cool.

4. Stir in the cheese, olives and yogurt and refrigerate for 30 minutes or until chilled.

Note: Do not freeze. This is *not* suitable for vegans.

HOT SLAW

Serves 4

Imperial (Metric):
10 oz (285g) white cabbage, finely shredded
1 small onion, peeled and finely chopped
1 carrot, peeled and grated
2 tablespoons chopped mixed nuts
4 tablespoons natural low-fat yogurt
1 tablespoon horseradish sauce
1 tablespoon mayonnaise
1 tablespoon finely chopped parsley

1. Mix the cabbage, onion, carrot and nuts in a large bowl. Cook on Full Power for 2 minutes. Stir, then cook for a further 2 minutes to slightly soften the vegetables.

2. Combine the yogurt, sauces and parsley in a jug and pour over the hot vegetables.

Note: This can be reheated but does not freeze well. It is only suitable for vegans if the sauces can be substituted. Silken tofu can replace the yogurt and grated horseradish the sauce.

KOHLRABI SALAD

Serves 4

Imperial (Metric):
12 oz (340g) kohlrabi
5 tablespoons mayonnaise
½ teaspoon celery seeds
1½ teaspoons fresh lemon juice
3 tablespoons pumpkin seeds

1. Cut the kohlrabi into quarters, put into a large bowl and cover with water.

2. Cover the bowl with vented plastic film and cook on Full Power for 6 minutes or until the water boils. Cover and cook for a further 9 to 10 minutes until just tender.

3. Drain, cool under cold running water, then peel, making sure that all the woody parts under the skin are removed. Cut into dice.

4. Mix together the mayonnaise, celery seeds, lemon juice and pumpkin seeds and stir in the kohlrabi.

Note: Do not freeze. This is *not* suitable for vegans unless vegan salad dressing is substituted.

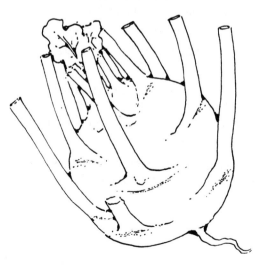

LETTUCE AND WALNUT SALAD

Serves 4

Imperial (Metric):
20-25 walnut halves
4 crisp round lettuce hearts
5 tablespoons natural yogurt
1½ teaspoons fresh lemon juice
Pinch sea salt
Pinch unrefined granulated sugar
1 teaspoon Dijon mustard
2 tablespoons freshly chopped parsley

1. Put the walnut halves in a small bowl, cover them with cold water and heat on Full Power for 2 minutes or until boiling. Drain.

2. Replace the walnuts in the bowl, cover with cold water and bring to the boil as before—the heating time will be slightly less. Drain.

3. Repeat the process once more (making three boilings in all), rinse the nuts under cold water, replace in a clean cool basin, cover with cold water and refrigerate for 3-4 hours. Drain and pat dry on kitchen paper.

4. Chop the walnuts and shred the lettuce.

5. In a salad bowl combine the yogurt, lemon juice, salt, sugar and mustard. Fold in the nuts and lettuce and sprinkle with the parsley.

Note: Do not freeze. This is *not* suitable for vegans.

PLANTERS SALAD

Serves 4-6

Imperial (Metric):
2 oz (55g) shelled peanuts
¼ teaspoon dried lovage
1 teaspoon fresh lemon juice
1 tablespoon fresh orange juice
1 tablespoon vegetable oil
Sea salt
Freshly milled black pepper
½ dessert apple, cored
1 lettuce heart, shredded
6 radishes, thinly sliced
6 spring onins, trimmed and finely sliced
1 small green pepper, cored, seeded and cut into strips

1. Spread the peanuts on a double sheet of greaseproof paper in the microwave and heat on Full Power for 4-5 minutes, occasionally tossing the nuts by lifting the edges of the paper until a nuttier flavour develops. The nuts become very hot so remove one with a spoon and leave to cool for a few seconds before testing.

2. In a salad bowl mix the lovage, citrus juices, oil and salt and pepper to taste.

3. Quarter and slice the apple and mix into the dressing, then add the remaining ingredients, not forgetting the chopped peanuts and their husks. Toss well.

Note: Do not freeze. This is suitable for vegans.

RUSSIAN SALAD

Serves 4

Imperial (Metric):
1 lettuce head, shredded
6 oz (170g) cooked potatoes
6 oz (170g) cooked carrots
2 oz (55g) cooked peas
2 oz (55g) cooked sliced green beans
5 tablespoons mayonnaise
2 tablespoons low fat natural yogurt
Sea salt
Freshly milled black pepper
Paprika

1. Arrange the shredded lettuce in individual bowls.

2. Dice the potatoes and carrots.

3. Mix the diced vegetables with the peas and beans and then mix in the mayonnaise and yogurt. Season to taste with salt and pepper.

4. Pile the mixture on to the lettuce and top with a sprinkling of paprika.

Note: Do not freeze. This is only suitable for vegans if a substitute dressing is available.

SPAGHETTI SALAD

Serves 4-6 as a main course.

Imperial (Metric):
8 oz (225g) wholemeal spaghetti
1-1½ pints (570-850ml) boiling water
1 teaspoon vegetable oil
1 teaspoon sea salt
6 oz (170g) button mushrooms
1 teaspoon fresh lemon juice
2 tablespoons soy sauce
2 tablespoons sesame seeds
Freshly milled black pepper

1. Break the spaghetti strands in half and put in a large bowl. Add boiling water to cover and stir in the oil and salt.

2. Cover and cook on Full Power for 4-5 minutes until boiling. Remove the cover, stir and cook for a further 4-5 minutes until boiling once more. Stir, cover tightly and leave to stand for 4-5 minutes until 'al dente.'

3. Drain and cool under cold running water. Drain and return to the bowl and chop up with kitchen scissors.

4. Finely slice the mushrooms and put into a large bowl. Stir in the lemon juice. Cover and cook on Full Power for 1½-2 minutes, stirring once during cooking, until just blanched.

5. Add the mushrooms with their juice, the soy sauce and sesame seeds to the spaghetti. Season with pepper, mix well and transfer to a serving dish. Chill slightly.

Note: Do not freeze. This is suitable for vegans.

SPINACH SALAD

Serves 4

Imperial (Metric):
1 lb (455g) fresh spinach
Pinch raw cane granulated sugar
Pinch sea salt
1 tablespoon sesame seed oil
2 tablespoons Tamari sauce
1 tablespoon cider vinegar
1 teaspoon French mustard
¼ teaspoon freshly milled black pepper
2 tablespoons sesame seeds, roasted

1. Wash the spinach in cold water and remove the thick stems.

2. Put the leaves with the water adhering to them in a roaster bag. Loosely seal with a rubber band, leaving a gap in the top for steam to escape.

3. Place the bag upright in the microwave and cook on Full Power for 3 minutes or until the leaves soften. Drain, pressing out all the surplus fluid. Pat with kitchen paper to dry, then coarsely shred the spinach leaves. Leave to cool. Put into a salad bowl.

4. Blend the sugar, salt, oil, sauce, vinegar, mustard, and pepper together. Pour over the spinach and toss to coat the leaves.

5. Scatter the sesame seeds on top.

Note: Do not freeze. This is suitable for vegans.

TOMATO SALAD

Serves 4

Imperial (Metric):
6-8 firm tomatoes
2 teaspoons fresh basil, chopped
Sea salt
Freshly milled black pepper
6 tablespoons olive oil
2 tablespoons red wine
½ teaspoon fresh lemon juice

1. Slice the tomatoes, put into a salad bowl and sprinkle with the basil, salt and pepper.

2. Put the wine and lemon juice into a small basin and cook on Full Power for 30 seconds. Leave to cool.

3. Mix the oil and reduced vinegar together and pour over the tomatoes. Regrigerate for 1 hour.

Note: Do not freeze. This is suitable for vegans.

TOMATO VEGETABLE RING

Serves 4-6

Imperial (Metric):
¾ pint (425ml) tomato juice
1½ teaspoons Gelozone or agar agar
1 teaspoon fresh lemon juice
1 tablespoon tomato purée
Salt and freshly milled pepper to taste
8 oz (225g) cooked mixed diced vegetables, cold

1. Pour ¼ pint (140ml) of the tomato juice into a large bowl and heat on Full Power for 1-2 minutes or until boiling. Stir in the agar agar until dissolved.

2. Add the remaining tomato juice, the lemon juice and tomato purée and season with salt and pepper.

3. Mix in the well-drained vegetables.

4. Rinse a 1 pint (570ml) ring mould with cold water and shake out the excess.

5. Spoon the mixture into the mould and leave to set in the refrigerator for at least 2 hours.

Note: Serve with a green salad. Do not freeze. This is suitable for vegans.

Main Courses

Choose one or more dishes from the recipes in this section and build your side dishes around them. Most are quite substantial and satisfying.

Select dishes of different colour and texture, perhaps including one containing pulses and another which has rice in it. If you fancy two dishes but both have a cheese topping, for example, just omit the topping from one of them.

When I am cooking for the family I am inclined to ignore the kitchen scales, which I faithfully use when wearing my author's hat. So long as you don't go mad and double the quantity of bulky ingredients, your cooking results should be all right. An extra tomato or slightly larger carrot is certainly not going to make much difference.

Most dishes can be partly or wholly cooked in advance, but when a recipe suggests browning under the grill, it is a good idea to complete this part after reheating. If you are using a plastic dish, however, remember that you can't put this under a hot grill. Egg dishes such as omelettes do not reheat well, but any egg left-overs will be passable if reheated on the Defrost/Low setting.

To give added interest and variety, include one or two dressed or plain vegetables with the main course.

ALMOND APRICOTINE STUFFED PITTAS

Serves 4

Imperial (Metric):
**8 oz (225g) dried apricots
½ pint (285ml) water
1 large onion, peeled and finely
chopped
½ oz (15g) butter or margarine
2 oz (55g) almonds, browned and
finely chopped
2 oz (55g) granary breadcrumbs
¼ pint (140ml) sweet red wine
Sea salt
Freshly milled black pepper
2 wholemeal pitta breads**

1. Put the apricots and water in a small bowl. Cover and cook on Full Power for 5 minutes until soft. Drain and leave to cool slightly.

2. Combine the onion and butter or margarine in a medium bowl. Cover and cook on Full Power for 3 minutes or until soft, stirring once during cooking.

3. Chop the apricots and add to the onion mixture.

4. Add the almonds, the breadcrumbs and the wine. Mix well and season lightly with salt and pepper.

5. Cover and cook on Full Power for 5 minutes, stirring occasionally until hot.

6. Heat the pittas on kitchen paper on Full Power for 30 seconds-1 minute. Cut in half, open the pockets and stuff with the mixture.

Note: The filling freezes well. Frozen pitta can be thawed and heated in the microwave but this takes a little longer. This is suitable for vegans if they substitute suitable margarine.

ASPARAGUS MOUSSE

Makes ¾ pint (340ml)
Serves 4-6

Imperial (Metric):
**1 × 12 oz (340g) can green asparagus
spears
1 tablespoon sunflower oil
2 teaspoons agar agar
½ oz (15g) wholemeal flour
4 oz (115g) drained silken tofu
½ teaspoon chopped chives
1 teaspoon fresh lemon juice
Sea salt
Freshly milled black pepper**

1. Drain the asparagus liquid into a small bowl and make up to ½ pint (285ml) with water.

2. Thoroughly stir in the oil, agar agar and flour. Cook on Full Power for 2 minutes, then whisk with a fork. Cook for a further 3 minutes, beating occasionally, until the sauce thickens.

3. Immediately pour into a blender and add the asparagus, tofu, chives, lemon juice, and salt and pepper to taste. Process to a purée, then pour into individual dishes. Refrigerate until set.

Note: Serve as a dip with crudités and wholemeal pitta bread fingers, or use as a sandwich spread mixed with chopped cucumber. Freezes but must be thawed at room temperature and be liquidized before serving. This is suitable for vegans.

AUBERGINE ROAST

Imperial (Metric):
1 lb (455g) aubergine
Pinch salt
1 teaspoon dried marjoram
1 small onion, finely chopped
1 garlic clove, peeled and crushed
1 teaspoon olive oil
1 egg
2 tablespoons skimmed milk powder
4 tablespoons fresh granary malt
brown breadcrumbs
½ teaspoon ground mace
Freshly milled black pepper

Topping:
2 tablespoons grated Parmesan
cheese
2 tablespoons fresh granary malt
brown breadcrumbs

1. Peel and slice the aubergine and put into a very large bowl with the salt and marjoram. Cover and cook on Full Power for 6-8 minutes until the aubergine is soft. Stir the mixture occasionally during cooking. Leave to stand, covered, while cooking the onion.

2. Put the onion, garlic and oil in a small basin, stir well, cover and cook on Full Power for 3 minutes.

3. Drain the aubergine and add to the blender with the onion mixture. Add the egg, milk powder, breadcrumbs, mace, and pepper to taste. Process to blend but not purée.

4. Spoon the mixture into a loaf-shaped dish that is suitable for the microwave. Reduce the setting to Defrost/Low and cook, uncovered, for 8-10 minutes until the loaf is set. Turn out on to a flameproof serving dish.

5. To make the topping, mix the

Parmesan cheese and breadcrumbs together. Sprinkle over the top of the loaf, then brown under the grill.

Note: Do not freeze. This is *not* suitable for vegans.

BEAN CURD AND MUSHROOMS PEKING STYLE

Serves 3-4

Imperial (Metric):
8 oz (225g) firm tofu, drained
1 tablespoon vegetable oil
8 oz (225g) mushrooms, sliced
2 tablespoons Hoisin sauce
Pinch cornflour
Freshly milled black pepper
1 tablespoon sesame seeds

1. Drain the tofu and pat dry with kitchen paper. Cut into eight or twelve equal-sized blocks.

2. Preheat a large browning dish to the maximum recommended by the manufacturers. Add the vegetable oil, then quickly put in the tofu pieces and cook uncovered on Full Power for 1 minute.

3. Turn the tofu pieces over and cook for a further 1 minute. Remove the tofu from the browning dish and set to one side.

4. Add the sliced mushrooms and Hoisin sauce and cornflour to the browning dish. Mix well, ensuring that the sauce is evenly distributed. Cover and cook on Full Power for 2 minutes or until the mushrooms are tender.

5. Return the tofu to the dish of mushrooms. Cover and cook on Full Power for 1 minute to reheat. Season to taste with pepper and sprinkle with sesame seeds. Serve with brown rice and a mixed salad.

Note: Do not freeze. This is suitable for vegans.

BEAN STUFFED VINE LEAVES

Imperial (Metric):
8 oz (225g) cooked black-eye beans
1 carrot
3 tablespoons tomato purée
½ teaspoon paprika
½ teaspoon thyme
Sea salt
Freshly milled black pepper
1 tablespoon Besan flour
8 vine leaves

1. Chop the beans and carrot in a food processor. Add the tomato purée, paprika, thyme and 4 tablespoons water. Season to taste with salt and pepper and process to a granular paste.

2. Put the mixture in a large bowl, cover and cook on Full Power for 4 minutes, stirring occasionally.

3. Stir the Besan flour into the mixture. Place one-eighth of the filling along one edge of each vine leaf. Roll up, tucking in the sides to form little parcels.

4. Arrange the parcels in a shallow dish. Pour over soy sherry sauce (see page 104), cover and heat on Full Power for 2 minutes or until hot.

Note: This freezes well. It is suitable for vegans.

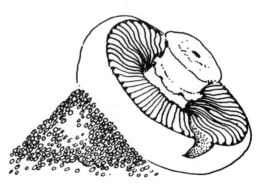

BELPORRI PUFFS

Makes 8

Imperial (Metric):

Puffs:
2½ oz (70g) wholemeal flour
2½ fl oz (70ml) water
1 oz (30g) polyunsaturated margarine
1 egg, beaten

Filling:
1 tablespoon oil
2 tablespoons wholemeal flour
¼ pint (140ml) milk
2 sticks celery, very finely chopped
½ oz (15g) hazelnuts, grated
Sea salt
Freshly milled black pepper

Topping:
¼ pint (140ml) tomato juice or
canned vegetable juice
2 teaspoons arrowroot

1. Sieve the wholemeal flour thoroughly, reserving the coarse bran.

2. Put the water and margarine in a jug and cook on Full Power for 1-1½ minutes until boiling rapidly. Quickly add the flour all at once and beat well with a fork.

3. Allow to cool slightly, then beat in the egg a little at a time. Put the paste into a piping bag fitted with a ½-inch (1½cm) plain nozzle. Pipe eight balls, well spaced out, on a greased baking sheet.

4. Bake in a preheated conventional oven at 425°F (220°C/Gas Mark 7) for 10 minutes, then reduce the temperature 375°F (190°C/Gas Mark 5) for 15 minutes until risen and golden brown.

5. Cool on a wire rack.

6. To make the filling, put the oil and wholemeal flour in a small bowl. Cook on Full Power for 45 seconds. Whisk in the milk. Cook on Full Power for 1 minute, whisking halfway through cooking.

7. Stir in the celery, hazelnuts and reserved bran. Cover and cook on Full Power for 5 minutes, stirring frequently. Season to taste with salt and pepper.

8. Slit the puffs and fill with the nut and celery mixture.

9. Mix 1 tablespoon of the tomato juice with the arrowroot, add to the remaining juice and cook on Full Power for 1½ minutes or until thickened. Stir frequently during cooking. Season to taste, then pour over the puffs and serve immediately.

Note: The puffs and the filling can both be frozen separately. The sauce should be freshly made. This is *not* suitable for vegans.

BORLOTTI SCALOPPINI

Serves 4

Imperial (Metric):
**1 lb (455g) potatoes
1 medium onion
1 tablespoon vegetable oil
12-14 oz (340-395g) cooked borlotti
beans
1 tablespoon tomato purée
1 tablespoon double cream
2 tablespoons water
Sea salt
Freshly milled black pepper
1 tablespoon chopped parsley**

1. Peel and finely slice the potatoes and onion.

2. Put the onion in a large bowl with the oil. Cover and cook on Full Power for 3 minutes to help to soften the onion.

3. Mix the sliced potatoes into the onion, tossing until well coated.

4. Reserve a few beans to garnish and mash the remainder with the tomato purée, cream and water. Season with salt and pepper.

5. Arrange half the potato and onion mixture in an 8-inch (20cm) round flameproof dish. Spread with the mashed beans and cover with the remaining potato and onion slices.

6. Cover and cook on Full Power for 12 minutes until the potatoes are tender.

7. Brown under a preheated grill, then garnish with the reserved borlotti beans and parsley.

Note: This freezes well, but should be browned and garnished after thawing and reheating on Full Power, turning the dish occasionally. It is suitable for vegans.

BROWNED VEGETABLE RICE IN SPICED YOGURT SAUCE

Imperial (Metric):
1 large onion, peeled and finely chopped
1 oz (30g) polyunsaturated margarine
1 medium carrot, scraped and diced
4 oz (115g) brown rice
4 oz (115g) peas
2 oz (55g) cut green beans
2 oz (55g) sweetcorn kernels
½ teaspoon sea salt
1 pint (570ml) hot vegetable stock
1½ teaspoons arrowroot
½ pint (285ml) thick-set natural yogurt
1 clove garlic, peeled and crushed
½ teaspoon turmeric
Pinch chilli powder
Pinch ground ginger
¼ teaspoon ground allspice
½ teaspoon sea salt

1. Put the onion and margarine into a medium bowl. Cover and cook on Full Power for 3 minutes until soft.

2. Place half the sautéed onion into another medium bowl and set aside.

3. Stir the carrot, rice, peas, green beans, sweetcorn, salt and stock into one of the onion mixture bowls. Cover and cook on Full Power for 30-35 minutes, stirring occasionally, until the rice is tender and most of the liquid is absorbed.

4. Cover tightly and stand for 10 minutes.

5. Meanwhile, blend the arrowroot with about 1 tablespoon of yogurt. Stir in to the remaining bowl of onion mixture. Add the garlic, turmeric, chilli powder, ginger, allspice, and salt. Cook on Full Power for 2 minutes. Stir.

6. Reduce the setting to Defrost/Low and cook for 3-4 minutes, stirring frequently to prevent boiling.

7. Pour the yogurt sauce over the hot rice.

Note: The rice mixture freezes well but the yogurt sauce should be freshly made. Only the sauce is unsuitable for vegans.

CARROT, CELERY AND BUTTER BEAN LASAGNE

Serves 4-5

Imperial (Metric):
6 sheets wholemeal lasagne
1 teaspoon sea salt
1 teaspoon vegetable oil

Purée:
1 lb (455g) carrots, cooked
½ head celery, cooked
Salt and freshly milled black pepper

Sauce:
1 pint (570ml) milk
6 black peppercorns
1 bay leaf
2 tablespoons sunflower oil
1 oz (30g) wholemeal flour
15 oz (425g) cooked butter beans

Garnish:
1 raw carrot, scraped and grated

1. Three-quarters fill a 2½-pint (1½ litre) casserole dish with hot water. Cook on Full Power until the water boils. Stir in 1 teaspoon salt and 1 teaspoon vegetable oil.

2. Lower two sheets of the lasagne into the water and cook on Full Power for 1

minute or until the water comes back to the boil. Add two more sheets of lasagne, bring to the boil, then add the remaining pasta sheets. Cook on Full Power for 5 minutes. Cover and leave to stand while heating the milk.

3. Combine the milk, peppercorns and bay leaf in a medium bowl and cook on Full Power for 3 minutes or until steaming. Leave to stand for 20 minutes to infuse.

4. Meanwhile, drain the cooked lasagne, separate the sheets on a clean greased worktop and cover with suitable plastic film.

5. Purée the carrots and the celery together to make the sauce and set aside.

6. Purée the butter beans in a liquidizer or blender.

7. Blend the oil and the flour together in a medium bowl and strain in the milk. Cook on Full Power for 3-4 minutes until a ring appears around the edge of the bowl. Whisk and continue cooking for a further 3 minutes, whisking twice during cooking. Mix in the puréed beans and season to taste.

8. Spread a layer of the butter bean sauce in the bottom of a 2½-pint (1½-litre) shallow oval dish. Cover with a layer of the carrot and celery mixture. Top with two sheets of lasagne side by side. Continue layering, finishing with the butter bean sauce.

9. Part cover and cook on Full Power for 6 minutes until the lasagne is cooked through and hot.

10. Garnish with grated raw carrot.

Note: This freezes but should be defrosted and reheated on the Defrost/Low setting. Vegans should use vegetable stock instead of milk.

WHOLE CARROTS

1. After peeling and scraping, place in a casserole. Whole carrots may have to be layered to fit into the casserole.

2. Add sufficient salted water to reach halfway up the vegetables. Cover and cook on Full Power, stirring occasionally.

3. Reposition carrots halfway through cooking, turning them over and transferring those that were underneath to the top. Allow 6-8 minutes for a small amount and 10-14 minutes for larger quantities.

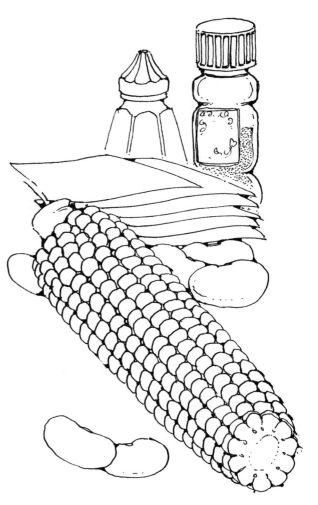

CARROT COCOTTES ON MARROW RINGS

Serves 4-6

Imperial (Metric):
1½ lb (680g) thick vegetable marrow, peeled
Sea salt
12 oz (340g) carrots, peeled and finely sliced
½ pint (285ml) milk
3 eggs at room temperature, beaten
¼ teaspoon mustard powder
Freshly milled black pepper

1. Remove the ends and cut the marrow into four or six thick slices and remove the centre pulp and seeds (these can be used in another recipe).

2. Put the marrow rings in a shallow dish, add 2 tablespoons water, cover and cook on Full Power for 8-10 minutes. Reposition the rings during cooking to ensure even results.

3. Remove the marrow with a slotted spoon. Add 3-4 tablespoons water and add salt to taste. Mix in the carrots, cover and cook on Full Power for 6 minutes or until soft. Drain and set aside.

4. Lightly oil 4-6 individual ramekin dishes.

5. Put the milk in a medium bowl and heat on Full Power for 1-2 minutes until warm. Beat in the eggs and mustard powder, and season to taste with salt and pepper. Divide the carrots between the dishes, then pour in the milk mixture.

6. Cover each ramekin with suitable plastic film and arrange in a circle in the microwave.

7. Cook on Full Power for 2 minutes, then give each dish a half-turn. Reduce the setting and cook on Defrost/Low for 5-7 minutes until just set.

8. Place the marrow rings on suitable serving plates and turn out the lightly set carrot cocottes into the middle. Reheat each plate on Full Power for 20 seconds.

Note: The cocottes can also be served cold. Do not freeze. This is *not* suitable for vegans.

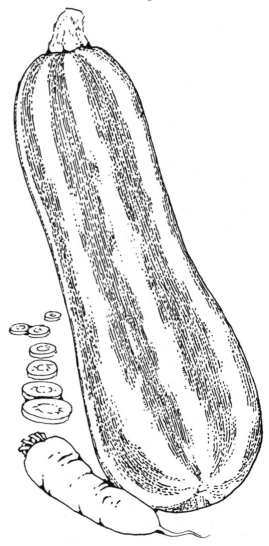

CAWL

Serves 4-6

Imperial (Metric):
1 oz (30g) butter or margarine
8 oz (225g) potatoes, peeled and cut up
1 large carrot, peeled and sliced lengthwise
2 small young turnips, peeled and diced
2 young parsnips, peeled and sliced
Sea salt
Freshly milled black pepper
1 medium leek, trimmed, washed and sliced
8 oz (225g) cooked or canned butter beans
1 pint (570ml) hot water
8 oz (225g) white cabbage
2 teaspoons arrowroot
2 oz (55g) grated cheese
Caraway seeds (optional)

1. Put the butter in a very large bowl and heat on Full Power for 30-45 seconds until melted.

2. Stir in the prepared potatoes, carrot, turnips and parsnips. Cover and cook on Full Power for 5-6 minutes, stirring occasionally. Season with sea salt and pepper.

3. Add the leek and beans and pour in the hot water. Cover and cook on Full Power for 15 minutes, stirring occasionally, until the vegetables are tender.

4. Separate the cabbage leaves and place on top of the other vegetables. Cover once more and cook for a further 5 minutes.

5. Using a slotted spoon, transfer the the vegetables to a heated serving dish, keeping the cabbage leaves on top.

6. Measure the liquid remaining in the bowl and cook uncovered on Full Power for 4-5 minutes until reduced to 8 fl oz (225ml). Blend the arrowroot with 2 tablespoons cold water, stir into the reduced liquor and cook on Full Power for 2 minutes, beating once during cooking.

7. Beat the cheese into the sauce. Pour over the hot vegetables and sprinkle with caraway seeds if liked.

Note: If the vegetables are not hot enough, heat uncovered on Full Power for a minute or two. Freeze the vegetables in the liquor but do not thicken until after thawing. Vegans should substitute vegetable fat and omit the cheese.

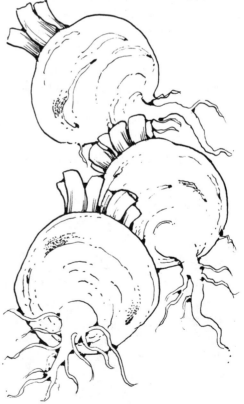

CELERY AND ALMOND CASSEROLE

Serves 4

Imperial (Metric):
1 head celery
5 tablespoons vegetable stock
1 oz (30g) flaked almonds
¼ teaspoon celery salt
¼ teaspoon sea salt
¼ teaspoon freshly milled black pepper
¼ oz (7g) polyunsaturated margarine
1 teaspoon potato flour

1. Rinse and trim the celery. Cut into 1-inch (2½cm)×½-inch (1cm) lengths.

2. Combine all the ingredients except the potato flour in a casserole. Cover and cook on Full Power for 12-15 minutes or until tender, stirring three times during cooking.

3. Mix the potato flour with 1 tablespoon of cold water. Stir into the casserole. Cook on Full Power for 30 seconds-1 minute, stirring frequently, until thickened.

Note: This freezes well. It is suitable for vegans.

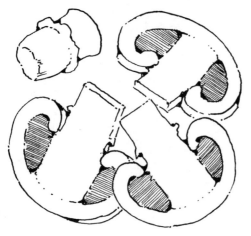

CELERY AND PEANUT LOAF

Serves 6

Imperial (Metric):
2 oz (55g) butter of margarine
1 large onion, peeled and finely chopped
1 celery stick, finely chopped
8 oz (225g) shelled peanuts, finely chopped and grated
1 carrot, peeled and grated
4 oz (115g) mushrooms, chopped
1 teaspoon Marmite
1 tablespoon bottled fruity sauce
½ pint (285ml) vegetable stock
3 oz (85g) porridge oats
Freshly milled black pepper
2 tablespoons Besan flour

1. Put the butter or margarine in a very large bowl. Cook on Full Power for 30 seconds or until melted.

2. Stir the onion and celery into the butter and cook on Full Power for 5 minutes, stirring once, until just beginning to brown.

3. Mix the peanuts into the softened vegetables. Cook on Full Power for 7 minutes until the roasted smell of the nuts is noticeable.

4. Add the carrot, mushrooms, Marmite, fruity sauce and stock. Cook on Full Power for 7 minutes or until the vegetables are soft. Stir twice during cooking.

5. Stir in the oats and season with pepper. Cook on Full Power for 3 minutes until the mixture is thick but mushy.

6. Mix in the Besan flour. Turn the mixture into a 1 lb (455g) loaf dish.

Cook on Full Power for 8-10 minutes until the loaf browns on top and begins to firm up. Leave for 10 minutes before turning out.

Note: Serve with tomato and sage or tomato and horseradish sauce. The loaf freezes well. Thaw and reheat on the Defrost/Low setting. It is suitable for vegans if vegetable fat is substituted for butter or margarine.

CHEESE AND VEGETABLE RAREBIT

Serves 4

Imperial (Metric):
6 oz (175g) grated Cheddar cheese
1 small onion, peeled and very finely chopped
1 medium carrot, peeled and grated
1 tablespoon bran
2 eggs
½ teaspoon mustard powder
2 tablespoons milk
Sea salt
Freshly milled black pepper
4 slices wholemeal bread, toasted

1. In a large bowl combine the cheese, onion, carrot, bran, eggs, mustard, and milk and season with the salt and pepper.

2. Cook on Full Power for 2 minutes, beating every 30 seconds until the mixture thickens.

3. Pile the cheese mixture on to the toast and brown under the grill if desired.

Note: Do not freeze. This is not suitable for vegans.

CHEESY RATATOUILLE

Serves 4

Imperial (Metric):
1 large onion
2 medium green peppers
1 medium red pepper
2 tablespoons vegetable oil
1 clove garlic, peeled and crushed
1 small courgette
3 tomatoes
½ teaspoon basil
2 tablespoons tomato purée
1 oz (30g) Cheddar cheese, grated
Sea salt
Freshly milled black pepper

1. Peel and finely chop the onion, de-seed and dice the peppers.

2. Combine the oil, onions, garlic and peppers in a large bowl. Cover and cook on Full Power for 5-6 minutes, stirring once.

3. Meanwhile trim and dice the courgette. Stir in to the pepper mixture, cover and cook on Full Power for 5-6 minutes until the vegetables are tender. Stir once or twice during cooking.

4. Chop the tomatoes and add to the cooked vegetables with the basil, tomato purée and cheese. Mix well, cover and cook on Full Power for 2 minutes. Season to taste.

Note: This dish freezes well, and freezing also improves its flavour. Vegans should omit the cheese.

CHICK PEA AND TAHINI CASSEROLE

Serves 6-8

Imperial (Metric):
Bunch spring onions, trimmed and sliced
2 medium carrots, peeled and thinly sliced
1 red pepper, cored, seeded and sliced
2 young parnips, peeled and cut into chunks
1 tablespoon olive oil
8 oz (225g) cooked chick peas
1 × 14 oz (395g) can tomatoes
Handful fresh parsley sprigs
2 tablespoons Tahini
Sea salt
Freshly milled black pepper

1. Put the spring onions, carrots, red pepper and parsnips into a large bowl or casserole.

2. Stir the oil into the vegetables, cover tightly and cook on Full Power for 10 minutes, stirring occasionally.

3. Add the chick peas, tomatoes and their juice and all the other ingredients, seasoning lightly with salt and pepper. Pour in ½ pint (285ml) boiling water. Cover and cook on Full Power for 20 minutes or until the vegetables are tender. Add additional salt and pepper if required.

Note: This freezes well but as the quantity is large, it is better to do this in measured servings. Thaw and reheat, covered, on Full Power, stirring occasionally. Suitable for vegans.

COURGETTE AND PEPPER QUICHE

Serves 4

Imperial (Metric):

Pastry
4 oz (115g) wholemeal flour
Pinch sea salt
½ teaspoon baking powder
1 tablespoon sesame seeds
2 oz (55g) polyunsaturated margarine
1 teaspoon vegetable oil
Approximately 3 tablespoons cold water

Filling:
1 red pepper, seeded and diced
4 oz (115g) courgettes, rinsed and finely sliced
2 spring onions, trimmed and finely sliced
1 tomato, chopped
2 eggs
1 tablespoon milk
Sea salt
Freshly milled black pepper

1. Mix the flour, salt, baking powder, and sesame seeds in a bowl.

2. Add the margarine and oil and blend in with a fork.

3. Add sufficient water to form a soft dough. The amount varies according to the absorbency of the flour.

4. Knead the dough lightly and wrap in cling film. Chill for 30 minutes.

5. Roll out the dough to fit a 6½-inch (17cm) round pie dish and cook on Full Power for 3-4 minutes, giving the dish a quarter-turn after each minute until the pastry is cooked.

6. To prepare the filling, put the diced pepper in a medium bowl, cover and cook on Full Power for 3 minutes.

7. Add the courgettes and onions and cook, covered, for a further 3 minutes. Spread the tomato in the pastry case and cover with the vegetables.

8. Beat the eggs and milk thoroughly together and season with salt and pepper. Pour over the vegetables. Reduce the setting to Defrost/Low and cook for 10 minutes. Cover with a circle of non-stick vegetable parchment and cook for a further 3-5 minutes until the centre is just set. Serve hot or cold.

Note: Do not freeze. This is *not* suitable for vegans.

CURD AND ALMOND PUFFS IN THICK CURRY SAUCE

Serves 4

Imperial (Metric):
2 pints (1.1 litres) milk
1 tablespoon lemon juice
½ oz (15g) ground almonds
½ teaspoon turmeric
¼ teaspoon sea salt

Sauce:
1 medium onion, peeled and very finely chopped
1 clove garlic, peeled and crushed
1 teaspoon vegetable oil
1 medium tomato, chopped
Pinch ground ginger
Pinch turmeric
¼ teaspoon ground cumin
¼ teaspoon ground coriander
Pinch chilli powder

1. Combine the milk and lemon juice in a large bowl and cook on Full Power for 10 minutes or until boiling. Cover and set aside for 30 minutes until thick curds form.

2. Strain this clabbered milk through clean muslin and squeeze as dry as possible. Discard the liquid.

3. Add the curd to the ground almonds, turmeric and salt and knead to a smooth paste. Shape into twelve small balls.

4. Deep-fry the balls in hot oil until light brown. Drain on kitchen pepper.

5. To make the sauce, combine the onion, garlic and oil in a small bowl, cover and cook on Full Power for 3 minutes or until soft.

6. Add all the remaining ingredients, stir in ¼ pint (140ml) water and purée in the liquidizer or blender. Pour back into the bowl and, without covering, cook on Full Power for 5 minutes, stirring occasionally until the sauce thickens.

7. Serve three curd puffs per person with a little of the sauce.

Note: Do not freeze the puffs, but the sauce freezes well. This is *not* suitable for vegans.

CURD CHEESE AND PINEAPPLE POTATOES

Serves 4-8

Imperial (Metric):
**4×6-8 oz (170-225g) jacket potatoes,
freshly cooked or reheated
8 oz (225g) curd cheese
4 thick slices fresh pineapple (about
2 oz (155g) each)
1 tablespoon toasted sunflower seeds
Sea salt
Freshly milled black pepper**

1. Halve the potatoes lengthwise and scoop out the pulp, making sure not to break the skins.

2. Mash the potato and mix in the cheese. Chop and add the pineapple and sunflower seeds and season to taste with salt and pepper.

3. Pile the filling into the potato skin, place in the microwave and heat on Full Power for 2-3 minutes.

Note: Do not freeze. This is *not* suitable for vegans.

CURRIED BEAN MEDLEY

Serves 4

Imperial (Metric):
**3 oz (85g) shallots, peeled and finely
chopped
1 tablespoon vegetable oil
3 tablespoons garam masala
1 teaspoon grated ginger root
1×14 oz (395g) can chopped
tomatoes
12 oz (340g) cooked mixed beans
Sea salt
Freshly milled black pepper**

1. Combine the shallots and oil in a casserole. Cover and cook on Full Power for 3-4 minutes until soft, stirring once during cooking.

2. Stir in the garam masala and grated ginger. Cover and cook on full power for 1 minute.

3. Stir in the chopped tomatoes. Cook, uncovered, on Full Power for 5 minutes or until the mixture is thick. Stir occasionally during cooking.

4. Add the beans and season with salt and pepper. Cover and cook on Full Power for 3-4 minutes, stirring occasionally, until the beans are hot.

Note: Serve with brown rice or Bulgur. This recipe freezes well. Canned mixed beans are now available in large supermarkets. They must be thoroughly rinsed before use and tend to be sweet. The dish is suitable for vegans.

DAHL SAG

Serves 4

Imperial (Metric):
**4 oz (115g) red lentils
1 small onion, peeled and finely
sliced
¾ pint (425ml) boiling water
1 green chilli
Juice of 1 lemon
12 oz (340g) cooked or thawed frozen
spinach
1 oz (30g) polyunsaturated margarine
Sea salt
Freshly milled blacked pepper
2-4 wholewheat pitta breads**

1. Rinse and drain the lentils.

2. Put the lentils and onion in a very large bowl and add the water. Three-

quarters cover and cook on Full Power for 10-15 minutes, stirring occasionally, until the lentils are soft.

3. Using gloves, de-seed and very finely chop the chilli. Stir into the lentils with the lemon juice, spinach and margarine. Season with salt and pepper.

4. Cook on Full Power for 15-20 minutes, stirring frequently, until the mixture is thick and just moist.

5. Warm the pitta breads on kitchen paper on Full Power for 30 seconds. Cut in half and fill the pockets with the mixture.

Note: The Dahl Sag freezes well. Pitta, which may be frozen separately, will take longer than stated to thaw and heat. The dish is suitable for vegans.

Deep Dish Spanish Omelette

Serves 4

Imperial (Metric):
1 medium onion, peeled
¼ green pepper, finely diced
1 small cooked potato, diced
2 tablespoons cooked peas
1 oz (30g) butter or margarine
8 tablespoons milk
4 eggs, beaten
2 oz (55g) Edam cheese, grated
Sea salt
Freshly milled black pepper
1 oz (25g) flaked almonds, browned

1. Put the onion in a small basin. Add 1 tablespoon water, cover and cook on Full Power for 4 minutes. Slice thinly. Put the onion, pepper, potato and peas in a 1 pint (570ml) straight-sided soufflé dish. Add the butter or margarine.

2. Cover and cook on Full Power for 2-3 minutes, stirring occasionally, until the vegetables are hot.

3. Stir in the milk and without covering cook for 30 seconds-1 minute until the milk is steaming but not boiling.

4. Mix in the eggs and cheese, and season with salt and pepper.

5. Reduce the setting to Defrost/Low. Cover and cook for 12-15 minutes, giving the dish a half-turn once during cooking.

6. Garnish with the almonds and serve hot with a green salad.

Note: Do not freeze. This is *not* suitable for vegans.

DEVILLED EGGS

Serves 1-4

Imperial (Metric):
**4 × ¼-inch (½cm) rings cut from the
centre of a large red pepper
1 large onion, peeled and very finely
chopped
1 clove garlic, peeled and crushed
2 tablespoons vegetable oil
4 tablespoons tomato purée
2 teaspoons French mustard
2 teaspoons mixed chopped fresh
herbs or ½ teaspoon mixed dried
herbs
Sea salt
Freshly milled black pepper
4 eggs**

1. Put the pepper rings on a plate, cover
and cook on Full Power for 1 minute to
soften. Set aside.

2. Put the onion, garlic and oil in a
shallow casserole dish. Cover with the lid
and cook on Full Power for 4-5 minutes,
stirring occasionally.

3. Stir in the tomato purée, mustard,
herbs and ¼ pint (140ml) water. Without
covering, cook on Full Power for 4-5
minutes, stirring occasionally, until the
sauce comes to the boil and is slightly
reduced. Stir in salt and pepper to taste.

4. Reheat the sauce for 30 seconds or
until bubbling, then arrange the pepper
rings in a single layer in the sauce and
break an egg into each—the yolk will
stay put although the white will spread.

5. Cover with the lid and cook on Full
Power for 1½-2½ minutes until the eggs
are just set. Leave for 30 seconds before
removing the lid. Serve with rice, pasta
or Lyonnaise potatoes.

Note: Do not freeze. This is not suitable
for vegans.

DOLMADES

Serves 4

Imperial (Metric):
**1 medium round lettuce
3 hard-boiled eggs, finely chopped
2 oz (60g) cooked brown rice
2 tablespoons mayonnaise
Salt
Freshly milled black pepper**

1. Trim and wash the lettuce leaves and
pat dry on a clean cloth. Pile eight
lettuce leaves on kitchen paper, place
them in the microwave, cover with
kitchen paper and heat on Full Power for
30 seconds until slightly softened.
Remove with a fish slice and repeat with
another batch of leaves. Press the stalks
to slightly flatten them. Chop the lettuce
heart.

2. Mix together the chopped lettuce,
eggs, rice and mayonnaise, and season to
taste with salt and pepper.

3. Layer two lettuce leaves together and
place a little of the egg mixture along
one edge. Roll up, tucking in the sides to
form a parcel. Repeat with the remaining
leaves and filling.

4. Arrange the lettuce parcels smooth-
side up in a small shallow dish. Cover
and cook on Full Power for 3-4 minutes
until hot. Give the dish a half-turn
halfway through cooking.

5. Serve the dolmades hot or cold with
a little of the cooking juices.

Note: Do not freeze. This is *not* suitable
for vegans.

EGG AND BAP LUNCH

Serves 4

Imperial (Metric):
4 wholemeal baps
1 oz (30g) butter or margarine
4 eggs
Sea salt
Freshly milled black pepper
¼ pint (140ml) soured cream
2 tablespoons chopped chives

1. Remove a round sliver of crust from the tops of the baps. Hollow out the soft bread centre. Set aside to make crumbs which can be stored in the freezer for future recipes.

2. Place dabs of butter or margarine in the hollows and arrange the baps in a circle of kitchen paper in the microwave. Cook uncovered on Full Power for 2-3 minutes until crisp, repositioning halfway through the cooking time.

3. Remove the kitchen paper. Break an egg into each of the crispy baps and season with salt and pepper.

4. Spoon soured cream over the eggs and space out in the microwave. Reduce the setting and cook uncovered on Defrost/Low for 6-7 minutes until the eggs are set. Give each bap a half-turn halfway through the cooking time and remove each bap as soon as the eggs are sufficiently cooked.

5. Garnish with chopped chives.

Note: Do not freeze. This dish cannot be adapted for vegans.

EGGS BENEDICT

Serves 4

Imperial (Metric):
2 oz (55g) polyunsaturated margarine
6 eggs
2 tablespoons fresh lemon juice
Sea salt
Freshly milled black pepper
4 slices wholemeal bread
Marmite

1. Put the margarine in a small bowl and heat on Full Power for 30 seconds or until melted.

2. Beat two of the eggs in with the lemon juice, then strain into the melted margarine and season with salt and pepper. Cook, uncovered, on Full Power for 45 seconds-1 minute, beating with a wire whisk every 10 seconds until the sauce thickens sufficiently to coat the back of a spoon. Do not overcook or the sauce will curdle. Cover and set aside.

3. Break the remaining eggs into individual oiled poachers or ramekin dishes. Cover each loosely with suitable plastic film and arrange in a circle in the microwave. Reduce the setting to Defrost/Low and cook for 5-7 minutes until the white is only just set, giving each dish a half-turn halfway through cooking.

4. Leave the eggs to stand, covered, while toasting the bread.

5. Spread the toast with Marmite. Slide an egg on to each and coat with the sauce. Serve at once.

Note: The sauce will freeze but must be thawed at the lowest setting and frequently stirred. This dish is *not* suitable for vegans.

INSALATA CALDA DI VIGNOLA

Serves 6

Imperial (Metric):
8 oz (225g) Bulgur cracked wheat
1 oz (30g) pine kernels
1 pint (570ml) boiling water
1 large onion
2 medium green peppers
2 tablespoons olive oil
1 clove garlic, crushed
3 tomatoes, chopped
½ teaspoon dry basil
Sea salt
Freshly milled black pepper

1. Put the cracked wheat and pine kernels in a large bowl. Cook, uncovered, on Full Power for 3 minutes, stirring once during cooking. This brings out the flavour. Stir in the boiling water. Cover and leave to stand for 15 minutes.

2. Meanwhile peel and chop the onion, de-seed and dice the peppers.

3. Mix the oil, onion, peppers and garlic together in a large bowl. Cover and cook on Full Power for 8-10 minutes until the vegetables are soft, stirring once during cooking.

4. Add the tomatoes and basil, cover and cook on Full Power for a further 1-2 minutes to soften the tomatoes.

5. Stir into the cracked wheat, which should have absorbed the water. Season with salt and pepper and reheat on Full Power for 2-3 minutes.

Note: This recipe freezes well. It is suitable for vegans.

LATKES

Makes 8 patties

Imperial (Metric):
2 medium onions
1½ lb (680g) potatoes
4 tablespoons chopped fresh parsley
2 eggs
2 oz (55g) wholemeal flour
Sea salt
Freshly milled black pepper
2 tablespoons vegetable oil

1. Peel and quarter the onions and potatoes. Grate coarsely by hand or in a food processor.

2. Mix in the parsley, eggs and flour and season well with salt and pepper.

3. Preheat a browning dish for the maximum time recommended by the manufacturers, adding 1 tablespoon of the oil during the last 30 seconds of the preheating time.

4. Using about half the mixture, place 4 large spoonsful in the dish. The mixture is fairly wet. Cook, uncovered, on Full Power for 3 minutes. Turn the patties over and cook for a further 2 minutes until the mixture is cooked through.

5. Transfer the patties to a serving dish and keep warm.

6. Reheat the browning dish on Full Power for 3 minutes. Add the remaining oil during the last 30 seconds and cook the remaining mixture.

Note: This freezes well. If preferred, the latkes can be cooked without the browning dish, by arranging them in the microwave on a circle of non-stick baking parchment, and then browning them in a frying pan afterwards. They are *not* suitable for vegans.

LEEKS MIMOSA

Serves 4-6

Imperial (Metric):
**2 hard-boiled eggs
6 medium leeks, each weighing
approximately 4 oz (120g), washed
and trimmed
½ pint (285ml) hot water
Milk
Salt
¾ oz (20g) polyunsaturated
margarine
¾ oz (20g) wholemeal flour
Sea salt
Freshly milled black pepper
2 tablespoons mayonnaise**

1. Separate the white and yolk of the eggs, chop the whites and sieve the yolks.

2. Arrange the leeks in a rectangular dish. Add ½ pint (285ml) hot salted water. Cover and cook on Full Power for 12 minutes, turning the leeks over and repositioning them halfway through cooking. Test and continue cooking if necessary.

3. Transfer the leeks to a warm serving dish.

4. Make up the cooking liquid to ½ pint (285ml) with milk.

5. Cook on Full Power for 1 minute, blend the margarine and flour together and stir in small amounts into the hot liquid. Cook for 1-2 minutes, stirring occasionally until thickened.

6. Season with salt and pepper and stir in the mayonnaise.

7. Spoon the sauce over the leeks and garnish with lines of chopped egg white and sieved yolk.

Note: Do not freeze. This is *not* suitable for vegans.

LENTIL CUTLETS

Makes 8

Imperial (Metric):
**8 oz (225g) split red lentils
1½ pints (850ml) hot water
2 bay leaves
1 medium onion, finely chopped
1 tablespoon vegetable oil
Sea salt
Freshly milled black pepper
4 tablespoons gram flour
Vegetable oil for frying**

1. Rinse the lentils and put into a very large bowl, add the water and bay leaves.

2. Cook, uncovered, on Full Power for 25-35 minutes. Stir occasionally at the beginning and more frequently towards the end of the cooking time. When cooked, the mixture will form a smooth paste when it is stirred.

3. Remove the bay leaves.

4. Combine the onion and the oil in a small bowl, cover and cook on Full Power for 4-5 minutes until soft.

5. Add the onion to the lentils, season and add the gram flour, mixing well.

6. With floured hands, shape the sticky mixture into eight patties. Cook four at a time in a lightly oiled preheated browning dish, allowing 1 minute on each side *or* shallow fry in a frying pan for 2½-3 minutes each side.

Note: These will freeze before or after cooking. Reheat on Full Power, repositioning the patties once. They are suitable for vegans.

LITTLE CHEESE AND CHERVIL POTS

Serves 4-6

Imperial (Metric):
8 oz (225g) cottage cheese
1 egg
12 chives, finely chopped
½ teaspoon dried chervil or 2 teaspoons fresh snipped chervil
2 teaspoons freshly chopped parsley
Pinch grated nutmeg
Sea salt
Freshly milled black pepper
4 tablespoons double cream, whipped

1. Combine the cottage cheese, egg, chives, chervil, parsley and nutmeg in the liquidizer or blender and process to a smooth paste. Season to taste with salt and pepper.

2. Divide the mixture between four or six individual ramekins, cover each loosely with cling-film, space out in the microwave and cook on Low/Defrost for 4 minutes. Give each dish a half-turn, then continue cooking for 2-3 more minutes or until only just set. Do not overcook or the outside will toughen and the mixture will curdle.

3. Leave to stand for 10 minutes, then carefully remove the cling-film and check that the middle is set. If necessary, return the ramekin to the microwave and cook on the lower possible setting (10%) for a further 30 seconds.

4. Top the pots with whipped cream and serve warm.

Note: Do not freeze. This is *not* suitable for vegans.

MULTI-COLOURED STUFFED PEPPERS

Serves 4

Imperial (Metric):
4×4-5 oz (115g-140g) peppers of assorted colours (red, green, yellow and black)
2 celery sticks
¼ oz (7g) butter or margarine
½ teaspoon Vecon
1×8 oz (225g) can tomatoes
6 oz (170g) cooked brown rice
4 tablespoons cooked chick peas
Sea salt
Freshly milled black pepper
4 tablespoons water
4 oz (115g) Cheddar cheese, grated

1. Remove the lids from the peppers and scraps out the seeds. Chop flesh from the pepper lids.

2. Rinse and finely chop the celery, put into a large bowl with the chopped pepper and the butter or margarine. Cover and cook on Full Power for 3 minutes or until the celery is crisp and tender.

3. Stir in the Vecon, then mix in the tomatoes, their juice, the rice and chick peas. Season with salt and pepper.

4. Press the stuffing into the peppers.

5. Stand the peppers in a shallow dish containing 4 tablespoons water. Cover and cook on Full Power for 8 minutes, then give each pepper a half turn. Re-cover and cook for a further 2-4 minutes or until the peppers are soft and the filling hot.

6. Top the peppers with the cheese and brown under the grill.

Note: Do not freeze. Vegans should use vegetable fat and omit the cheese.

MUSHROOM AND BEAN MOUSSAKA

Serves 4

Imperial (Metric):
8 oz (225g) button mushrooms
2 oz (55g) soft margarine
1 shallot, peeled and very finely chopped
3 oz (85g) brown rice
13 fl oz (375ml) hot water
Pinch sea salt
1 oz (30g) wholemeal flour
½ pint (285ml) milk
4 oz (115g) Cheddar cheese, grated
4 oz (115g) cooked kidney beans

1. Wipe the mushrooms. Cut off the stalks level with the caps. Chop the stalks and set the caps aside.

2. Put 1 oz (30g) of the margarine in a 2 pint (1.1 litre) casserole and add the shallot. Cook on Full Power for 1 minute, stirring once during cooking. Mix in the chopped mushroom stalks and cook for a further minute.

3. Add the rice, water and salt to the casserole. Cover, leaving a small gap for steam to escape. Cook on Full Power for 15-18 minutes until the rice is just tender. Stir quickly, then replace the lid tightly and leave to stand.

4. Put the remaining margarine in a small bowl and heat for 20 seconds or until melted. Stir in the flour and cook for a further 30 seconds until the roux is puffy.

5. Stir the milk into the roux and cook on Full Power for 3½-4 minutes until the sauce thickens, whisking every 1½ minutes and at the end of cooking.

6. Stir three-quarters of the cheese into the sauce and season with salt and pepper.

7. Pour a little of the sauce into a flameproof soufflé dish and arrange the mushroom caps on top. Pour a few more spoons of sauce over the mushrooms. Cover with the beans and then the rice. Smooth the surface and pour over the remaining sauce. Without covering, cook on Full Power for 5 to 6 minutes until the mixture is hot.

8. Sprinkle the remaining cheese over the surface and brown under the grill.

Note: Do not freeze. This is *not* suitable for vegans.

MUSHROOMS IN GARLIC SAUCE

Serves 4

Imperial (Metric):
**1 lb (455g) button mushrooms
1 clove garlic
¼ teaspoon sea salt
3 oz (85g) butter or margarine
Freshly milled black pepper
4 slices wholemeal bread
1 teaspoon arrowroot
1 tablespoon water
2 tablespoons freshly chopped
parsley**

1. Quarter any large mushrooms.

2. Crush the garlic and salt together with a knife.

3. Put the butter or margarine into a large bowl. Heat on Full Power for 1 minute. Stir until melted.

4. Add the mushrooms, garlic and pepper to taste. Toss the mushrooms to coat with the butter mixture. Cook on Full Power for 5 minutes, stirring occasionally until the mushrooms are tender but not soft.

5. While the mushrooms are cooking, toast the bread.

6. Using a slotted spoon, pile the cooked mushrooms on to the hot toast.

7. Blend the arrowroot with 1 tablespoon cold water and stir into the remaining juices. Cook for 1 minute or until thickened, stirring once during and once after cooking.

8. Pour the sauce over the mushrooms, sprinkle with parsley and serve hot.

Note: Do not freeze. Vegans should substitute suitable fat.

NUT PAELLA

Serves 6-8

Imperial (Metric):
**Few strands saffron
8 oz (225g) brown rice
1 × 14 oz (395g) can tomatoes
½ tablespoon sunflower oil
½ green pepper, cored, seeded and
cut into strips
½ red pepper, cored, seeded and cut
into strips
1 onion, peeled and finely chopped
2 oz (55g) lightly roasted pine kernels
2 oz (55g) lightly roasted cashew nuts
1 teaspoon Holbrook's sauce
½ teaspoon dried basil
Pinch bayleaf powder
Sea salt and freshly milled black
pepper**

1. In a very large bowl, soak the saffron strands in ½ pint (285ml) boiling water. Leave to stand for 10 minutes.

2. Add the rice. Pour on an additional 1½ pint (850ml) boiling water. Stir in the tomatoes and their juice. Cook on Full Power for 35-45 minutes, stirring once during cooking, until the rice is cooked and nearly dry (the tomatoes will rise to the top of the rice).

3. Put the oil, peppers and onion in a medium bowl. Cover and cook on Full Power for 5 minutes or until soft.

4. Add the sautéed vegetables, the nuts, sauce, basil, and bayleaf powder to the rice and season to taste. Mix carefully. Cover and vent and cook on Full Power for 5 minutes to reheat. Stir before serving.

Note: This freezes well. It is suitable for vegans.

PARSNIP PATTIES

Serves 4-6

Imperial (Metric):
1½ lb (680g) parsnips
1 teaspoon lemon juice
2 oz (55g) butter
1 egg, lightly beaten
Sea salt
Freshly milled black pepper
3 oz (85g) toasted hazelnuts, finely grated

1. Peel the parsnips, and halve and remove the woody cores if using old parsnips. Roughly chop and put in a very large bowl. Cover with approximately ½ pint (285ml) salted water. Stir in the lemon juice. Cover and cook on Full Power for 13 minutes or until soft, stirring occasionaly.

2. Drain and mash the cooked parsnips with a potato masher. Beat in the butter and egg. Season to taste with salt and pepper.

3. Shape the mixture into six patties— the mixture is rather wet at this stage but it is workable. Spread the hazelnuts on a sheet of non-stick vegetable parchment or cling-film. Stand the patties on the nuts, then turn them over and coat with the aid of a palette knife.

4. Arrange the patties on a large shallow dish. Cook on Full Power for 4 minutes. Serve with lemon and parsley sauce (page 102) or tomato and sage sauce (page 104).

Note: This freezes well. Thaw and reheat on Full Power. It is *not* suitable for vegans.

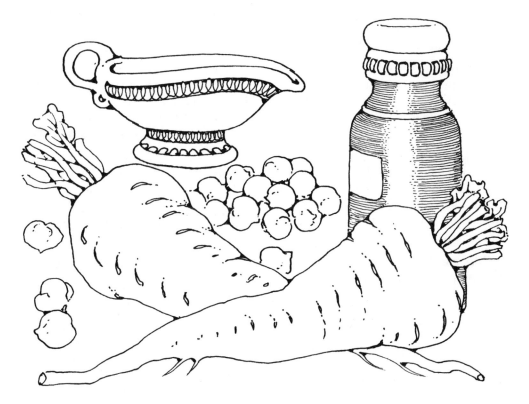

PEPPER AND ONION STUFFED CRISPY POTATOES

Serves 4

Imperial (Metric):
2 × 10 oz (285g) baking potatoes
1 tablespoon vegetable oil
1 small green pepper, cored, seeded and diced
1 small onion, peeled and chopped
1 clove garlic, peeled and crushed
Pinch ground ginger
Pinch saffron powder
Sea salt
Freshly milled black pepper
1 tablespoon freshly chopped parsley

1. Wash and dry the potatoes and prick deeply with a fork. Place on pieces of kitchen paper and cook on Full Power for 5 minutes.

2. Reposition and turn the potatoes over, then continue cooking for 5-6 minutes until soft. Cut in half lengthways and scoop out the pulp. Mash lightly with a fork.

3. Arrange the potato skins in a shallow dish and pour a little of the oil around the inside. Brush the remaining oil over the outside of the skins. Cook on Full Power for 4-6 minutes until the skins are crispy, removing each skin as it is ready.

4. Mix together in a small bowl the green pepper, onion, garlic, ginger and saffron and season to taste with salt and pepper. Cover tightly and cook on Full Power for 3-4 minutes until soft.

5. Mix the cooked vegetables into the mashed potato then pile the mixture into the potato skins. Reheat, uncovered, for 2-3 minutes until hot. Sprinkle with the chopped parsley.

Note: Do not freeze. This is suitable for vegans.

PUFFY OMELETTE WITH PIMIENTO SAUCE

Serves 2

Imperial (Metric):
1 teaspoon vegetable oil
1 × 6¾ oz (190g) can pimientoes, drained
1 teaspoon tomato purée
1 tablespoon pine kernels
3 eggs, separated
Sea salt
Freshly milled black pepper

1. Lightly oil a 9-inch (22cm) shallow round dish and line the base with a disc of non-stick vegetable parchment.

2. Purée the pimientoes, tomato purée and nuts together in the liquidizer or blender. Pour into a small bowl and cook on Full Power for 2 minutes until piping hot, stirring occasionally. Cover and keep warm.

3. Using grease-free beaters, whisk the egg whites until stiff.

4. In another large bowl, whisk the egg yolks with 3 tablespoons cold water and salt and pepper to taste.

5. Stir 1 tablespoon of the beaten white into the yolks, then gently fold in the remainder.

6. Pour the egg mixture into the prepared dish, reduce the setting to Defrost/Low and cook for 5-8 minutes or until just set. Give the dish a quarter-turn every minute during cooking.

7. Remove the dish from the microwave, leave to stand for 1 minute, then turn out on to a flameproof dish, and gently fold the omelette over.

8. While the omelette is standing, prepare a hot grill. Raise the microwave setting and reheat the sauce for 1 minute.

9. Brown the omelette under the grill, pour the sauce over and serve at once.

Note: The sauce may be frozen but the omelette must be freshly cooked. When preparing the recipe for 4 people, double the sauce ingredients and increase the cooking and reheating times by 1 minute at each stage. Prepare the omelette ingredients together but cook each omelette separately. This is not suitable for vegans.

SAVOURY KASHA

Serves 6

Imperial (Metric):
4 celery sticks
1 oz (30g) butter
4 oz (115g) roast buckwheat
2 oz (55g) cashew nuts
2 cardamon pods, bruised
¼ teaspoon ground cloves
½ teaspoon celery seeds
18 fl oz (515ml) hot vegetable stock
Sea salt
Freshly milled black pepper

1. Finely slice the celery and put in a casserole with the butter. Cover and cook on Full Power for 5 minutes, stirring occasionally until just tender.

2. Stir in the buckwheat and nuts. Cover and cook on Full Power for 4 minutes, stirring once.

3. Add the remaining ingredients and season with salt and pepper.

4. Cover and cook on Full Power for 15 minutes, stirring once during cooking. Leave to stand, covered, for 5 minutes, then if necessary uncover and cook for a further 3-4 minutes until all the liquid is absorbed.

5. Serve hot or cold.

Note: This dish freezes well. Vegans should substitute vegetable fat for the butter.

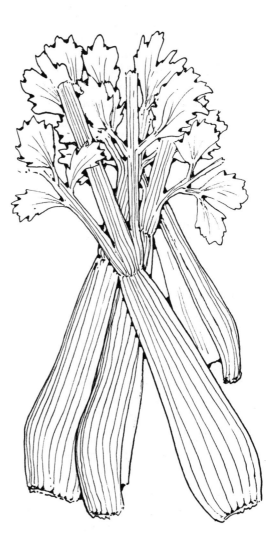

SOYA BEAN CASSEROLE WITH CRUNCHY TOPPING

Serves 4

Imperial (Metric):
3 tablespoons vegetable oil
4 tablespoons fresh wholemeal breadcrumbs
1 medium onion, peeled and finely chopped
1 clove garlic, peeled and crushed
1 × 14 oz (395g) can tomatoes
1 teaspoon dried basil
½ teaspoon dried oregano
Sea salt
Freshly milled black pepper
2 tablespoons wholemeal flour
1 tablespoon polyunsaturated margarine
1 lb (455g) cooked soya beans

1. Put 2 tablespoons of the oil in a shallow dish. Heat on Full Power for 1 minute.

2. Stir in the breadcrumbs and cook uncovered for 2½-3 minutes, stirring frequently until crispy.

3. In a medium bowl, combine the chopped onion, the garlic and the remaining tablespoon of the oil. Cover and cook on Full Power for 3 minutes until soft, stirring once during cooking.

4. Add the tomatoes and their juice, the basil, oregano and a light sprinkling of salt and pepper. Three-quarters cover and cook on Full Power for 5 minutes.

5. Blend the flour and margarine together and whisk the paste into the tomato mixture a little at a time.

6. Cook, uncovered, on Full Power for 3 minutes to thicken, lightly stirring twice during the cooking period.

7. Purée the mixture in the liquidizer or blender.

8. Put the beans in a casserole. Pour over the sauce. Cover and cook on Full power for 3 minutes, stirring occasionally until hot.

9. Sprinkle with the crumbs and serve hot.

Note: Both the casserole and the crumbs freeze well but should be stored and thawed separately. Vegans should use vegetable fat.

SPECIAL RAREBIT EN CROÛTE

Serves 4

Imperial (Metric):
4 slices wholemeal bread
3 tablespoons vegetable oil
Trace garlic powder
1 small red pepper, seeded and cut up
¼ small onion, peeled and cut up
¼ teaspoon potato flour
4 oz (150g) Emmenthal cheese, grated
1 egg yolk
Pinch mustard powder
Few drops Holbrook's sauce
Pinch freshly milled black pepper
2 cocktail gherkins, finely chopped
1 tablespoon water

1. Trim the crusts from the bread.

2. Mix together the oil and garlic powder in a shallow dish. Heat on Full Power for 2 minutes.

3. Quickly dip the bread into the oil, making sure that both sides are coated. Arrange in a circle in the microwave, on

non-stick vegetable parchment or directly on the turntable or base.

4. Cook on Full Power for 1 minute. Carefully turn the slices over. The bread will be soft and soggy. Cook on Full Power for 2½-3 minutes, repositioning every minute until the bread is crisp. Remove each piece as soon as it becomes crisp—overcooked croûte will burn. Drain on kitchen paper.

5. Purée the pepper and onion in a liquidizer or blender. Set aside.

6. Mix together the potato flour, cheese, egg yolk, mustard, Holbrook's sauce, black pepper, chopped gherkins, and water in a bowl. Cook on Full Power for 1 minute to melt the cheese and lightly cook the mixture. Stir once during cooking.

7. Pile the cheesy mixture on to the croûtes and spoon a little red pepper and onion purée on top. Arrange in a circle in the microwave and cook, uncovered, for 1-2 minutes until hot. Serve at once.

Note: Do not freeze. If preferred, cut the bread with fancy cutters or into fingers before making into croûtes. Serve as appetizers or at a buffet. This is not suitable for vegans.

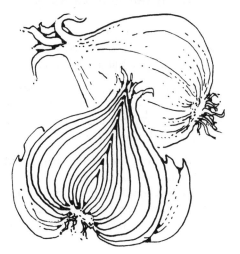

SPICED TOFU

Serves 4

Imperial (Metric):
1 teaspoon corn oil
1 garlic clove, finely chopped
1-inch (2½cm) fresh ginger, finely chopped
1 large onion, finely chopped
½ red pepper, cut into strips
½ teaspoon ground coriander
½ teaspoon garam masala
¼ teaspoon ground cumin
8 oz (225g) firm tofu, diced into 1-inch (2½cm) cubes
3 oz (85g) cashew nuts, grated
¼ teaspoon ground cardamom
Sea salt and freshly milled black pepper to taste
1 teaspoon wholemeal flour
¼ pint (140ml) cold vegetable stock

1. Gather all the ingredients together first because speed is essential to maintain the maximum heat during cooking.

2. Preheat the browning dish to the maximum recommended by the manufacturers. Immediately add the oil and stir in the garlic, ginger, onion, red pepper, ground coriander, garam masala, and cumin. Cook on Full Power for 2 minutes, stirring once during cooking.

3. Add the tofu, immediately turning the pieces over. Add the cashew nuts and cardamom. Cover and cook on Full Power for 2 minutes. Season to taste with salt and pepper.

4. Blend the flour and vegetable stock together and pour over the tofu. Cook on Full Power for 2 minutes or until boiling. Serve hot on a bed of rice.

Note: This will not freeze. It is suitable for vegans.

SPINACH AND RED PEPPER GRATINÉE

Serves 4

Imperial (Metric):
1 lb (455g) spinach, tough stalks removed
2 red peppers, cored, seeded and cut into thin strips
4 celery sticks, thinly sliced
2 medium onions, peeled and finely chopped
1 oz (30g) sultanas, chopped
¼ teaspoon sweet paprika
Generous pinch raw cane sugar
Pinch ground cinnamon
1 teaspoon sea salt
4 tablespoons tomato purée
1 tablespoon arrowroot
5 oz (140g) drained silken tofu
4 tablespoons fresh wholemeal breadcrumbs

1. Wash the spinach in plenty of cold water and shake off the excess moisture.

2. Put the spinach in a roasting bag and seal loosely with an elastic band, leaving a gap for steam to escape.

3. Put the bag upright in the microwave and cook on Full Power for 5-6 minutes until the leaves pack down. Drain, reserving the liquid. Set the spinach aside.

4. Put the peppers, celery and onion into a shallow casserole, cover tightly and cook on Full Power for 15 minutes, stirring several times during cooking.

5. Mix together the sultanas, paprika, sugar, cinnamon, salt, tomato purée, arrowroot, and approximately 2 tablespoons reserved spinach liquor, and cook on Full Power for 2-3 minutes,
stirring occasionally until thickened. Stir into the vegetables, then cover and cook for 2 minutes.

6. Layer the spinach and mixed vegetables in a flameproof dish.

7. Beat the tofu and 3 tablespoons of the crumbs together and spread over the vegetables. Sprinkle with the remaining crumbs.

8. Brown under the grill.

Note: May be frozen without the topping. This is suitable for vegans.

SPINACH MILLES FEUILLES

Serves 4

Imperial (Metric):
8 oz (225g) frozen puff pastry, firm but thawed
12 oz (340g) spinach leaves
1 tablespoon vegetable oil
2 oz (55g) wholemeal flour
½ pint (285ml) milk
¼ teaspoon nutmeg powder
Sea salt
Freshly milled black pepper

1. Roll out the pastry to a 9-inch (22½cm) circle. Trim the edges with a sharp knife. Chill for 15 minutes.

2. Put the pastry circle on to a sheet of kitchen paper. Cook on Full Power for 5-6 minutes until the pastry rises and no longer shivers.

3. Remove from the kitchen paper and brown the top of the pastry under a preheated grill, taking care not to burn as it will brown very quickly. Cool on a rack.

4. When cool, trim the edges and split in half horizontally.

5. Rinse the spinach and shake off excess moisture. Put into a roasting bag, loosely sealed at the top with a small rubber band or put into a lidded casserole. Cook on Full Power for 5 minutes until the spinach is tender. Drain well and purée the spinach in a liquidizer or blender.

6. To make the filling, mix the oil, flour, milk, nutmeg and spinach purée in a large bowl and season with salt and pepper. Cook on Full Power for 4-5 minutes, stirring frequently until very thick.

7. Fill the puff pastry case with the spinach filling. Serve hot or cold.

Note: The filling freezes well but it is best to cook pastry freshly. This is *not* suitable for vegans unless plant milk is substituted and the pastry is made with vegetable fat.

TACOS PUEBLO

Serves 4

Imperial (Metric):
4 oz (115g) cooked red kidney beans
2 oz (55g) butter or margarine
Dash Tabasco
1 green pepper, cored and seeded
4 oz (115g) beansprouts
4 oz (115g) grated Cheddar cheese
8 taco shells
1 onion, peeled and cut into thin rings

1. Put the beans, butter or margarine and Tabasco in a large bowl. Cover and cook on Full Power for 4-5 minutes, stirring occasionally until the beans are hot. Mash roughly with a potato masher so that most of the beans are broken.

2. Cut the pepper into strips and put in a dish. Cover and cook on Full Power for 1 minute to soften slightly. Drain.

3. Mix the pepper strips and beansprouts with the kidney beans and half the cheese.

4. Fill the taco shells with the bean mixture but do not compress.

5. Place the filled tacos close together and open side up in a dish which just fits and, without covering, heat on Full Power for 2 minutes or until the tacos are hot.

6. Transfer to serving plates and garnish with the remaining cheese and onion rings.

Note: Do not freeze. These are *not* suitable for vegans unless the cheese is omitted and vegetable fat substituted for butter.

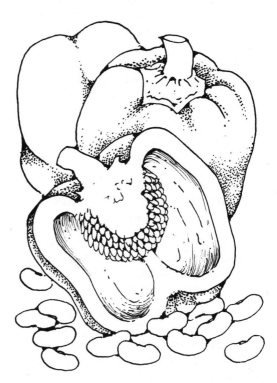

TAGLIATELLE VERDI WITH SOURED CREAM AND CHIVE SAUCE

Serves 4

Imperial (Metric):
8 oz (225g) dried green tagliatelle
½ teaspoon sunflower oil
Sea salt

Sauce:
2 oz (55g) polyunsaturated margarine
1 egg yolk
¼ pint (140ml) soured cream
1 teaspoon fresh lemon juice
Sea salt
Freshly milled black pepper
1 tablespoon chopped chives

1. Put the tagliatelle into a large casserole and add about 1½ pints (850ml) rapidly boiling water to reach 1-2 inches (2½-5cm) above the pasta. Stir in the oil and salt to taste. Cook on Full Power for 5 minutes, the stir, taking care not to break up the pasta. Cook for a further 2-3 minutes until the pasta is nearly tender, then cover with the lid and leave to stand for 5 minutes while preparing the sauce.

2. Put the margarine in a small bowl and heat on Full Power for 30 seconds or until melted.

3. Stir together the egg yolk, soured cream and lemon juice and strain into the melted margarine. This is to remove the egg threads.

4. Cook on Full Power for 1 minute, whisking every 20 seconds, then continue cooking for a further ½-1 minute, whisking every 10 seconds until the sauce thickens sufficiently to coat the back of a spoon. Season to taste with salt and pepper and stir in the chives.

5. Drain the tagliatelle, return it to the casserole dish and mix in the sauce. Serve immediately.

Note: Do not freeze. This is *not* suitable for vegans.

TOFU PANCAKES WITH BEANSPROUTS

Makes 4

Imperial (Metric):
1 × 10½ oz (297g) packet silken tofu, drained
7 tablespoons fresh malted brown (granary) breadcrumbs
2 oz (55g) Brazil nuts, finely grated
1 tablespoon soy sauce
4 oz (115g) sprouted mung beans

1. Using a fork, mash the tofu in a large bowl. Thoroughly mix in the breadcrumbs, nuts and soy sauce.

2. Spread about 4 tablespoons of the mixture in a pancake shape on to a piece of greased foil and brown the top under a preheated grill (about 5 minutes). Remove the foil and pancake with a fish slice and leave to cool. Meanwhile cook three more pancakes.

3. Invert the pancakes on to suitable plates so that the unbrowned side is uppermost.

4. Arrange 1 oz (30g) of sprouted beans along the centre of each pancake. Fold over, tucking one edge underneath.

5. Replace in the microwave and heat on Full Power for 45 seconds—1 minute for each pancake.

Note: Do not freeze. This is suitable for vegans.

TOFU SATAY

Serves 3

Imperial (Metric):
1 lb (455g) firm tofu, cut into ½-inch cubes

Marinade:
1 tablespoon corn oil
1 tablespoon soy sauce
1 tablespoon lemon juice
2 teaspoons turmeric
¼ teaspoon mustard powder
1 garlic clove, crushed
1 small onion, finely chopped

Sauce:
1 pint (570ml) vegetable stock
5 spring onions, sliced
2 garlic cloves, peeled but whole
3 bay leaves
5 cardamom pods, bruised
1-inch (2½cm) piece cinnamon stick
2 tablespoons lemon juice
2 tablespoons clear honey
2 teaspoons curry powder
1 oz (30g) desiccated coconut
6 oz (170g) salted peanuts, finely crushed

1. Combine the marinade ingredients together in a medium bowl. Carefully mix in the tofu to avoid breaking up. Ensure that the tofu is well coated with marinade. Cover and marinate in the refrigerator for a minimum of 2 hours, but preferably overnight.

2. To make the sauce, combine all the ingredients except the peanuts in a medium bowl. Cook on Full Power for 15 minutes until the liquid is reduced to two-thirds. Strain, reserving the liquid.

3. Add the crushed peanuts to the reduced liquid and stir well. Cook on Full Power for 8 minutes or until the sauce thickens. Stir twice during cooking.

4. Using a slotted spoon, transfer the tofu to a casserole dish. Discard the marinade. Pour the sauce over the tofu, cover and heat on Full Power for 3 minutes.

Note: Do not freeze. This is suitable for vegans.

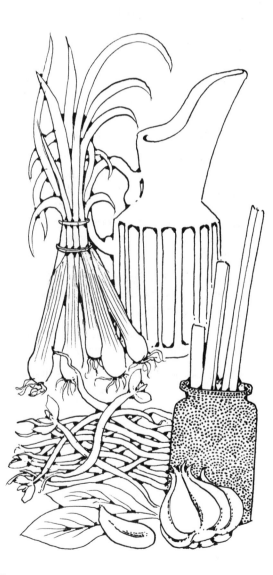

TOMATO AND OLIVE SHIR

Serves 4

Imperial (Metric):
4 slices wholemeal bread, toasted
1 small onion
3 medium tomatoes
12 pitted black olives
½ oz (15g) butter
6 eggs, lightly beaten
Sea salt
Freshly milled black pepper

1. Toast the bread and keep it warm.

2. Peel and finely chop the onion. Skin and chop the tomatoes. Reserve half the olives and chop the remainder.

3. Combine the onion and butter in a medium bowl. Cover and cook on Full Power for 3 minutes or until soft, stirring once during cooking. Mix in the eggs and tomatoes, beating thoroughly with a fork. Season to taste with salt and pepper and stir in the chopped olives.

4. Cook on Full Power for 4-6 minutes, beating every minute until the eggs are scrambled, but still soft.

5. Pile on to the toast and garnish with the remaining olives.

Note: Do not freeze. This is *not* suitable for vegans.

TOMATOES FLORENTINE EN CROÛTE

Serves 4

Imperial (Metric):
4 slices wholemeal bread
2 tablespoons vegetable oil
¼ teaspoon paprika
2 Moroccan (beef) tomatoes
2 oz (55g) chopped cooked or frozen chopped spinach
1 egg, beaten
1 tablespoon grated Parmesan cheese
1 tablespoon fresh wholemeal breadcrumbs
1 teaspoon tomato purée
Sea salt
Freshly milled black pepper
Pinch dried marjoram
¼ teaspoon cornflour
¼ teaspoon tomato purée
¼ teaspoon fruity sauce

1. Cut out a circle from each bread slice, using the largest cutter that will fit inside the crusts. Remove the centre of each bread circle with a smaller cutter to leave a ½-inch (1cm) bracelet. Do not use a wooden board as the cutters may scrape dust on to the bread. Cover the work surfaces with non-stick paper.

2. Put the oil and paprika into a large rectangular dish and heat on Full Power for 2 minutes. Carefully lower the bread bracelets into the oil and cook on Full Power for 1½ minutes. Turn the bracelets over—but take care as they will be very soft. Cook for a further 1½ minutes or until they crispen. Drain on kitchen paper.

3. Halve the tomatoes and scoop out the pulp.

4. Roughly chop the tomato pulp and mix in a large bowl with the spinach, egg, Parmesan, breadcrumbs and 1 teaspoon tomato purée. Season to taste with salt and pepper, then mix in the marjoram. Cook on Full Power for 1 minute, then beat thoroughly.

5. Spoon the filling into the tomato shells and arrange in a circle in a shallow dish. Reduce the setting to Defrost/Low and cook for 3 minutes. Carefully give each tomato a half-turn, then continue cooking for a further 4-5 minutes until the tomato wells soften.

6. Using two tablespoons, place a tomato half in each croûte. Keep warm.

7. Stir the cornflour, ¼ teaspoon tomato purée and the fruity sauce into the juices remaining in the dish and cook on Full Power for 45 seconds to thicken. Stir thoroughly, then place a spoonful of the sauce on top of each tomato. Serve hot.

Note: Do not freeze. This is *not* suitable for vegans.

VEGETABLE CURRY

Serves 4

Imperial (Metric):
**Small onion, peeled and finely chopped
1 tablespoon vegetable oil
4 cardamoms, bruised
1 teaspoon fenugreek seeds
½ teaspoon mustard seeds
1 teaspoon coriander seeds
1 tablespoon turmeric
1 large potato, peeled and diced
2 medium courgettes, cut into 1-inch (2½cm) chunks
1 small cauliflower, stalks removed and florets divided up**

**4 oz (115g) cut green beans
1×8 oz (225g) can tomatoes
2 bay leaves
¼-½ pint (140-285ml) hot water
½ teaspoon salt
¼ teaspoon freshly milled black pepper**

1. Put the onion into a very large bowl with the oil. Cook on Full Power for 4 minutes until the onions begin to brown.

2. Add the cardamoms, fenugreek, mustard, coriander seeds and turmeric. Cook on Full Power for 1 minute, stirring halfway through cooking.

3. Add the diced potato to the mixture. Cover and cook on Full Power for 3 minutes, stirring twice.

4. Add the courgettes, cauliflower florets, beans, tomatoes and bay leaves.

5. Cover and cook on Full Power for 5 minutes.

6. Add about half the water. Cover and cook for 10 minutes. Reduce the setting to Defrost/Low and cook for 15 minutes, stirring occasionally, until the vegetables are tender, adding the remaining water if necessary. Adjust seasoning to taste.

Note: This improves with freezing. It is suitable for vegans.

Walnut and Aubergine Gratin

Serves 6

Imperial (Metric):
**2 medium aubergines, rinsed and
stalks removed
2 oz (55g) shelled walnuts, roughly
chopped**

Sauce:
**1 tablespoon walnut oil
1 tablespoon sunflower oil
1 oz (30g) wholemeal flour
½ pint (285ml) milk
Salt and freshly milled black pepper
2 oz (55g) grated Cheddar cheese
1 tablespoon grated Parmesan cheese
6 medium tomatoes, sliced
2 level teaspoons dried oregano**

Topping:
**2 tablespoons wholemeal
breadcrumbs
1 tablespoon grated Parmesan cheese**

1. Slice the unpeeled aubergines and put into a very large bowl together with the walnuts. Add 2 pints (1.1 litre) cold water. Cover and cook on Full Power for 12-14 minutes until boiling.

2. Drain thoroughly and repeat the process, using 1 pint (570ml) cold water, and cook on Full Power for 10 minutes or until boiling. Drain thoroughly.

3. Put the walnut and sunflower oils into a small bowl, stir in the flour, add the milk and mix thoroughly. Cook on Full Power for 2 minutes, then beat with a whisk and cook for a further 1-2 minutes until a thickened band appears around the edge. Beat again. Season to taste with salt and pepper.

4. Add the grated Cheddar and 1 tablespoon of Parmesan cheese to the sauce. Mix well to melt the cheese.

5. Put a layer of the aubergine and nut mixture into the bottom of a 2-pint/1.1 litre flameproof dish. Top with half the tomatoes, half the oregano and half the sauce. Layer the remainder in the same way, finishing with the sauce.

6. Reduce the setting and cook on Defrost/Low for 15 minutes, giving the dish a half-turn halfway through cooking, until the aubergine is tender.

7. To make the topping, mix together the breadcrumbs and Parmesan cheese.

8. Sprinkle the topping over the sauce and cover with non-stick vegetable parchment.

9. Raise the setting and cook on Full Power for 4-5 minutes, then uncover and brown under the grill if desired.

Note: This freezes well but the topping should be frozen separately. Thaw on the Defrost/Low setting for 20-25 minutes before adding the topping and completing the recipe. It is *not* suitable for vegans.

DRESSED AND ACCOMPANYING DISHES

Dressed vegetables is a very old-fashioned term to describe vegetables that are garnished or served in a sauce. They can be served on their own as light supper dishes or as lunch snacks, as they do not sit heavily on the stomach. Provided they complement one another, they can be put together to provide a more varied meal and you can serve them with fresh salad, rice or pasta, or prepare them as an accompaniment to the main dishes.

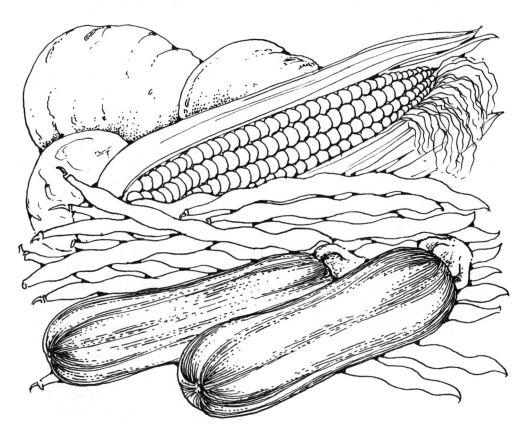

BHINDI IN TAMARIND

Serves 4

Imperial (Metric):
1 lb (455g) okra or ladies fingers
1×8 oz (225g) can chopped tomatoes
**4 spring onions, peeled, trimmed
and finely sliced**
**¼ teaspoon tamarind concentrate or
two pieces dried tamarind**
Sea salt
Freshly milled black pepper
1 teaspoon cornflour
1 tablespoon cold water

1. Wash, top and tail the okra, place in a casserole and add the tomatoes and their juice, the onions, tamarind and a light seasoning of salt and pepper. Mix well, then cover with the lid and cook on Full Power for 10 minutes, stirring occasionally.

2. Remove the lid and cook for a further 5 minutes, stirring twice during cooking.

3. Using a slotted spoon, transfer the okra to a warmed serving dish.

4. Blend the cornflour and cold water together and stir into the cooking liquor. Cook on Full Power for 1 minute, then stir vigorously. Pour the sauce over the okra and serve hot with cooked roast buckwheat or lentils.

Note: Freezes adequately. Tamarind concentrate is obtainable from grocers selling Indian, African or Caribbean foods. It is made from the tamarind fruit which resembles prunes and is sour to the taste but improves flavours. This dish is suitable for vegans.

BOULES DE POMMES DE TERRE

Serves 4

Imperial (Metric):
4 oz (115g) goat's cheese
**4 tablespoons double cream, half
whipped**
2 oz (55g) polyunsaturated margarine
1 egg, beaten
1 lb (455g) mashed potatoes
Sea salt
Freshly milled black pepper
2 oz (55g) grated Emmental cheese

1. Mash the goat's cheese with half the cream, all the margarine and the egg. Mix with the potatoes and season with salt and pepper.

2. With wet hands, shape the mixture into eight balls.

3. Half fill a medium bowl with boiling water and heat on Full Power until fast-boiling once more. This should take only a few minutes.

4. Lower four of the potato balls into the water, making sure they are well spaced out. Cook on Full Power for 1-2 minutes until they rise to the surface. Transfer with a slotted spoon to a flameproof dish or plate.

5. Bring the water in the bowl back to the boil in the microwave and cook the remaining potato balls.

6. Spoon dabs of the remaining cream on the potato balls and sprinkle with the grated Emmental. Brown under a preheated grill.

Note: This freezes well. This recipe is *not* suitable for vegans or vegetarians who do not eat the cheese specified.

BRUSSELS SPROUTS WITH CHESTNUTS

Serves 4

Imperial (Metric):
12 fresh chestnuts
1 lb (455g) Brussels sprouts, trimmed
and rinsed (fresh or frozen)
½ oz (15g) butter

1. To cook the chestnuts, split deeply through the shells and put into the microwave oven. Cook on Full power for 1 minute. Reposition the nuts and continue cooking, checking every 10 seconds so that you remove the nuts as they become ready. The nuts will feel very hot. Shell and skin them as soon as possible, and cut them up.

2. Put the Brussels sprouts in a casserole with about 6 tablespoons salted water. Cover and cook on Full Power for 8 minutes or until the sprouts are tender. Drain and replace in the casserole.

3. Add the butter and nuts to the sprouts. Cover and cook on Full Power for 3 minutes, stirring once during cooking. Leave to stand for a minute or two before serving.

Note: Do not freeze if frozen sprouts are used. Vegans should substitute vegetable fat for the butter.

CHINESE-STYLE BEANS

Serves 4

Imperial (Metric):
1 lb (455g) French beans
2-inch (5cm) piece root ginger
½ oz (15g) butter or margarine
Sea salt
Freshly milled black pepper
¼ pint (140ml) water

1. Top and tail the beans. Peel and coarsely grate the ginger.

2. Put the butter or margarine into a casserole dish, heat on Full Power for 20-30 seconds to melt. Season with salt and pepper.

3. Stir the beans and ginger into the melted butter. Cover and cook on Full Power for 4 minutes, stirring twice during cooking.

4. Add the water. Cover and cook on Full Power for 4-6 minutes until tender, stirring occasionally.

5. Remove the beans to a serving dish with a slotted spoon and keep warm. Cook the liquor uncovered on Full Power for 2-5 minutes until only 1 tablespoon remains. Pour over the beans and serve immediately.

Note: Do not freeze as it is the freshness that makes this dish so delicious. It is suitable for vegans if vegetable fat is substituted.

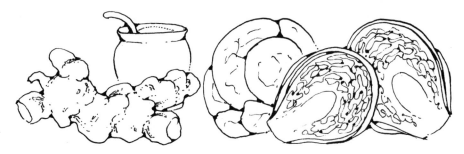

COURGETTES NOUVELLE

Serves 3-4

Imperial (Metric):
1 lb (455g) (7 medium) courgettes
½ teaspoon sea salt
1 large or 3 small spring onions
1 tablespoon sunflower oil
½ teaspoon ground nutmeg
Freshly milled black pepper
6-8 outer leaves from a cos lettuce,
coarsely shredded

1. Top and tail the courgettes but do not peel. Grate finely, put on a plate, sprinkle with milled sea salt, cover and set aside for 30 minutes.

2. Finely slice the spring onions, put into a medium casserole and stir in the oil. Cook on Full Power for 2 minutes, stirring once during cooking. Add the nutmeg and a shake of pepper.

3. Mix in the lettuce and cook on Full Power for 2-3 minutes.

4. Drain the courgettes. Squeeze out the remaining juices by hand. Add to the lettuce and cover and cook on Full Power for 2½-3½ minutes until just tender, stirring occasionally. Leave to stand, covered, for 2 minutes before serving hot.

Note: This will freeze but the cooking time after adding the courgettes should be halved. It is suitable for vegans.

CREAMED CHICORY

Serves 4

Imperial (Metric):
1 lb (455g) chicory (8 small heads)
½ oz (15g) butter
2 teaspoons fresh lemon juice
2 tablespoons double cream
2 tablespoons natural yogurt
Sea salt
Freshly milled black pepper
Cress to garnish

1. Trim the stalk ends of the chicory and wipe the leaves. Put the whole heads of chicory into a casserole with the butter and lemon juice. Cover with the lid and cook on Full Power for 8-10 minutes until just tender, repositioning the chicory heads once during cooking.

2. Drain and remove the chicory. Combine the cream and yogurt in the casserole and season with salt and pepper.

3. Return the chicory to the casserole and toss to coat with the sauce. Cover and heat on Full Power for 30 seconds only.

4. Serve garnished with cress.

Note: Do not freeze. Vegans should substitute vegetable fat for the butter and omit the cream and yogurt.

CREAMED SWEETCORN AND MUNG BEANS

Serves 4

Imperial (Metric):
**1 small shallot, peeled and finely
chopped
1 tablespoon vegetable oil
8 oz (225g) frozen sweetcorn kernels
¼ teaspoon ground allspice
Sea salt
Freshly milled black pepper
2 fl oz (55ml) set natural yogurt
6 oz (170g) sprouted mung beans**

1. Mix the shallot and oil together in a medium casserole, cover and cook on Full Power for 3 minutes or until the shallot is soft.

2. Stir in the sweetcorn, allspice and salt and pepper to taste. Cover and cook on Full Power for 4 minutes, stirring once during cooking.

3. Stir the yogurt into the sweetcorn and mix in the beansprouts.

4. Without covering cook on Full Power for 1-1½ minutes until hot. Do not overheat or the yogurt may curdle. Stir before serving.

Note: Do not freeze. This is *not* suitable for vegans.

FRESH ASPARAGUS WITH SOURED CREAM SAUCE

Serves 3-4

Imperial (Metric):
**1 lb (455g) asparagus
¼ teaspoon sunflower oil
¼ pint (140ml) soured cream
½ teaspoon fresh lemon juice
Sea salt
Freshly milled black pepper**

1. Remove the tough ends from the asparagus, then pare or scrape the stalks.

2. Arrange the asparagus in two layers in a rectangular casserole so that half the stalks point in one direction and the other half in the other. Smaller spears should be placed in the centre.

3. Add ¼ pint (140ml) of water mixed with the oil, cover and cook for 9-14 minutes on Full Power until the tips are just tender (cooking time depends upon the size of the asparagus). Leave covered while making the sauce.

4. Stir the lemon juice into the cream and season with salt and pepper.

5. Serve the drained asparagus hot or cold with a little of the sauce.

Note: Fresh asparagus may be frozen but it is much nicer when freshly cooked. The sauce is not suitable for vegans but they can substitute vinaigrette.

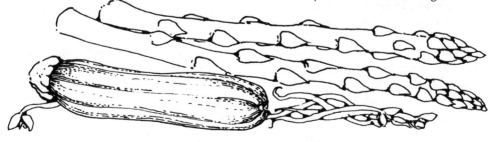

FRIED RICE

Imperial (Metric):
2 tablespoons vegetable oil
1 large onion, peeled and very finely chopped
12 oz (340g) cooked brown rice
2 eggs (optional)
1 oz (30g) other ingredients such as diced peppers, nuts, cooked chick peas
1 tablespoon soy sauce
Freshly milled black pepper

1. Put the oil and onion into a large bowl. Cook on Full Power for 4-5 minutes until the onion is soft. Stir occasionally during cooking.

2. Stir in the rice and cook for 5 minutes or until the rice is hot, stirring occasionally during heating.

3. Add the remaining ingredients and cook for a further minute.

Note: This will freeze if the eggs are omitted. It is suitable for vegans without the eggs.

GLOBE ARTICHOKES HOLLANDAISE

Serves 4

Imperial (Metric):
4 well rounded globe artichokes
½ pint (285ml) hot water
1 teaspoon lemon juice

1. Remove the tips from the leaves and the long stems from the base of the artichokes. Wash the artichokes thoroughly.

2. Combine the water and lemon juice in a large deep casserole and arrange the artichokes bottom ends towards the outside. Cover tightly and cook on Full Power for 10 minutes.

3. Reposition the artichokes, turning them over as well as round, replace the cover and cook for a further 10 minutes until a leaf pulls away easily.

4. Leave to stand, covered, for 5 minutes before serving.

Note: Serve hot with hollandaise sauce (see page 101). Artichokes can be served cold with vinaigrette if liked. Vegans can use the recipe for low calorie sauce on page 105.

HOT CHILLI RUNNERS

Serves 3-4

Imperial (Metric):
1 fresh green chilli
1 lb (455g) young runner beans
3 tablespoons tomato purée
¼ teaspoon ground cinnamon
Sea salt
Freshly milled black pepper
2 teaspoons cornflour
1 tablespoon freshly chopped coriander leaves

1. Put the chilli into a small basin and add cold water to cover. Cook on Full Power for 2 minutes or until boiling, then reduce the setting to Defrost/Low and cook for a further 5 minutes. Lift the chilli out with tongs and put on to a board. Use a knife and fork to remove the seeds, then slice paper-thin.

2. Top and tail the beans and remove the strings from the sides. Thinly slice diagonally.

3. Combine the beans, tomato purée, cinnamon and sliced chilli in a large casserole. Add ½ pint (285ml) water.

Season to taste with salt and pepper.

4. Cover with the lid, raise the setting and cook on Full Power for 15-17 minutes or until the beans are tender. Stir occasionally during cooking.

5. Blend the cornflour with 2-3 tablespoons cold water and stir into the beans. Without covering, cook on Full Power for 5 minutes, stirring occasionally until the sauce thickens and thickly coats the beans. Serve garnished with parsley.

Note: This freezes well without the parsley garnish. It is suitable for vegans.

HOT CUCUMBER IN LEMON VERBENA

Serves 4

Imperial (Metric):
1 large cucumber
2 spring onions, trimmed and finely sliced
1 tablespoon vegetable oil
3 tablespoons wholemeal plain flour
¼ pint (140ml) vegetable stock
Sea salt
Freshly milled black pepper
1 teaspoon dried lemon verbena
Lemon slices to garnish

1. Peel the cucumber and reserve the peel. Cut the cucumber into half lengthwise, then into ½-inch (2cm) chunks, cover and put into a dish.

2. Combine the spring onions and oil in a medium bowl, cover and cook on Full Power for 2 minutes until the onions soften.

3. Stir the flour and then the stock into the onions and cook for 2 minutes,

whisking once during and once after cooking. Season to taste with salt and pepper.

4. Mix in the lemon verbena. Chop and add the cucumber peel.

5. Reduce the setting to Defrost/Low, cover and cook for 6-8 minutes, stirring once during cooking.

6. Purée in the liquidizer or blender and adjust the seasoning if necessary.

7. Cook the cucumber chunks, covered, for 2 minutes on Full Power until hot but not soft.

8. Pour the sauce over the cucumber and cook, uncovered, for a further minute. Garnish with lemon slices.

Note: Do not freeze. This is suitable for vegans.

LEEK PURÉE

Serves 4

Imperial (Metric):
1 lb (455g) leeks
¼ pint (140ml) salted water
Freshly milled black pepper

1. Wash, trim and finely slice the leeks.

2. Put the leeks in a casserole with the water. Season with pepper, cover and cook on Full Power for 6 minutes or until the leeks are tender.

3. Without draining, purée in the liquidizer or blender.

4. Cover and reheat on Full Power for 1-2 minutes until hot. Serve immediately.

Note: This freezes well, is versatile and can be used as a vegetable, a sauce or as a filling. It is suitable for vegans.

LETTUCE IN CUCUMBER SAUCE

Serves 4

Imperial (Metric):
1 iceberg lettuce
4 tablespoons chopped chives
¼ pint (140ml) milk
¼ pint (140ml) water
½ vegetable stock cube
1 small onion, peeled and cut in half
Sea salt
Freshly milled black pepper
1 oz (30g) butter or margarine
1 oz (30g) wholemeal flour
1 large cucumber, cut into small chunks

1. Remove and discard any damaged outer leaves of the lettuce. Cut into four wedges.

2. Put the lettuce and chives on a suitable serving dish, cover with kitchen paper and cook on Full Power for 3-4 minutes until tender but not collapsed. Set aside.

3. Combine the milk, water, crumbled stock cube and onion in a jug. Season with salt and pepper. Cook on Full Power for 2 minutes until hot, but not boiling. Cover and set aside for 30 minutes to infuse.

4. Remove and discard the onion. Put the butter in a medium bowl. Heat on Full Power for 20-30 seconds to melt. Stir in the flour and cook on Full Power for 1 minute to cook the roux.

5. Whisk in the milk and cook on Full Power for 1½-2 minutes until the sauce thickens. Whisk every 30 seconds during cooking.

6. Purée the cucumber and sauce together in the liquidizer or blender.

7. Pour back into the bowl. Cook on Full Power for 1 minute. Stir, then reduce the setting to Defrost/Low and continue cooking for 10 minutes, stirring occasionally.

8. Pour the cucumber sauce over the lettuce. Cook on Full Power for 1-2 minutes or until hot.

Note: Do not freeze. Vegans should substitute vegetable fat and milk.

LYONNAISE POTATOES

Serves 4

Imperial (Metric):
1 oz (30g) vegetable margarine
1 medium onion, peeled and very finely chopped
Sea salt
Freshly milled black pepper
1 tablespoon freshly chopped parsley
1 lb (455g) potatoes

1. Put the margarine in a very large bowl and heat for 30 seconds or until melted.

2. Stir the onion into the margarine and season with salt and pepper. Cover and cook for 3-4 minutes, stirring occasionally, until the onions are soft. Mix in the parsley.

3. Peel the potatoes and slice very thinly, preferably in a food processor. Toss in a clean cloth to dry.

4. Tip the potatoes into the onion mixture, adding them a few at a time and stirring well so that all the slices are coated.

5. Transfer the mixture to a shallow round flameproof dish. Arrange the top layer in overlapping order. Cover with a

plate or plastic film and cook on Full Power for 10-12 minutes or until the potatoes are tender.

6. Remove the cover and brown the surface, putting the dish about 4 inches (10cm) below a hot grill.

Note: This can be frozen but it tends to discolour. It is suitable for vegans.

MARROW RINGS

Serves 4 as a vegetable, and 2 as a light lunch dish

Imperial (Metric):
1½ lb (750g) vegetable marrow
½ oz (15g) butter or margarine
1 teaspoon Marmite or Vecon
1 tablespoon double cream
½ teaspoon arrowroot
Sea salt
Freshly milled black pepper

1. Wash and peel the marrow, and slice into ½-inch (1cm) rings. Do not remove the pulp and seeds, which are both edible and appetizing. Arrange in a single or double layer in a casserole and dot with the butter or margarine. Cover and cook on Full Power for 10-12 minutes, repositioning the slices during cooking to ensure that all are ready at the same time.

2. Using a slotted spoon, transfer the marrow slices to a hot serving dish. Stir the Marmite or Vecon and cream into the juices, then blend in the arrowroot.

3. Cook the sauce on Full Power for 20-30 seconds to slightly thicken. Stir thoroughly and season to taste with salt and pepper.

4. Pour the sauce over the marrow and serve hot.

Note: The marrow and juices freeze well. Complete stages 2 and 3 after thawing and reheating. This is *not* suitable for vegans.

MUSHROOMS À LA GRECQUE

Serves 4

Imperial (Metric):
2 tablespoons olive oil
3 tablespoons red wine
2 tablespoons water
1 tablespoon fresh lemon juice
1 tablespoon chopped onion
10 black peppercorns
Pinch fennel seeds
Pinch coriander seeds
½ teaspoon sea salt
1 lb (455g) button mushrooms
Fresh chopped parsley to garnish

1. Mix together in a very large bowl the oil, wine, water, lemon juice, onion, peppercorns, fennel, coriander seeds, and salt.

2. Cover and cook on Full Power for 2 minutes to heat the liquid and infuse the spices.

3. Quarter any large mushrooms. Stir into the hot liquid to lightly soften the mushrooms. Cover and cook on Full Power for 5 minutes. Stir thoroughly and then leave for 5 minutes.

4. Transfer the mushrooms to a serving dish with a slotted spoon.

5. Cook the liquid, uncovered, on Full Power for 2-3 minutes until reduced to about 3 tablespoons. Strain over the mushrooms and chill for several hours.

6. Garnish with parsley.

Note: Do not freeze. This is suitable for vegans.

NUTMEAT DUMPLINGS

Makes 12 dumplings

Imperial (Metric):
1 oz (30g) butter or margarine
2 oz (55g) wholemeal flour
1 oz (30g) wholemeal breadcrumbs
1 oz (30g) hazelnuts, grated
1 teaspoon baking powder
Sea salt and freshly milled black
pepper
1 egg, beaten

1. Rub butter or margarine into the flour. Mix in the breadcrumbs, hazelnuts and baking powder. Season to taste with salt and pepper.

2. Add the beaten egg, mixing well. Shape the mixture into twelve small balls.

3. Drop the dumplings into a large bowl of boiling water or add to a vegetable casserole. Cover and vent and cook on Full Power for 5 minutes.

4. Remove with a slotted spoon and serve with tomato and horseradish sauce or a vegetable casserole.

Note: These dumpling absorb about ¾ pint (425ml) liquid during cooking. If you wish to add them to a vegetable casserole, the extra liquid will be required. Serve hot or cold. Freeze if necessary. This is *not* suitable for vegans.

PILAU RICE

Serves 4-6

Imperial (Metric):
1 oz (30g) butter or margarine
1 small onion, peeled and finely
chopped
6 oz (170g) brown rice
2-3 oz (55-85g) other additional
ingredients such as chopped red or
green peppers, crushed garlic clove,
cashew nuts, sultanas, peas,
sweetcorn and sliced mushrooms
1½ pints (850ml) hot vegetable stock
½ teaspoon freshly milled black
pepper
Sea salt

1. Put the butter or margarine in a 3-pint (1¾-litre) casserole and add the onion. Cook on Full Power for 3 minutes or until the onion glistens. Stir occasionally during cooking.

2. Add the rice and cook for 1-1½ minutes.

3. Add the remaining ingredients except the salt. Cover and cook on Full Power for 35-40 minutes, stirring once during cooking. Quickly stir, then replace the lid and leave to stand for 10 minutes.

4. Check for cooking, adding a little more water and giving additional cooking time if necessary.

5. Add salt to taste.

Note: Basic pilau will freeze provided the added ingredients are freezable. Vegans should substitute suitable fat for the butter or margarine.

POACHED FENNEL

Serves 4

Imperial (Metric):
2 large fennel bulbs
1 tablespoon fresh lemon juice
¼ teaspoon freshly milled black pepper
1 teaspoon fennel seeds
1 teaspoon vegetable oil
Sea salt

1. Wash the fennel, remove a slice from the bottom and discard the outer leaves if necessary. Chop the fennel stalks. Cut each bulb into six or eight wedges.

2. Mix the stalks, lemon juice, pepper, fennel seeds, and oil in a casserole and add 4 tablespoons salted water.

3. Arrange the fennel wedges in the mixture. Cover with the lid and cook on Full Power for 12 minutes, repositioning the wedges once during cooking.

4. Leave to stand for 3-4 minutes, then drain and serve hot.

Note: Freezes well. This is suitable for vegans.

POTATOES FROM GUJARAT

Serves 4

Imperial (Metric):
3 × 8 oz (225g) baking potatoes
1 medium onion
1 teaspoon vegetable oil
1 × 14 oz (395g) can tomatoes
1-inch (2½cm) piece ginger root
2 garlic cloves, peeled
½ teaspoon turmeric
½ teaspoon ground cumin

½ teaspoon sea salt
¼ teaspoon chilli compound powder
¼ teaspoon freshly milled black pepper
¼ teaspoon cinnamon
Curry leaves to garnish

1. Wash and prick the potatoes. Arrange in a circle on kitchen paper in the microwave oven and cook on Full Power for 10 minutes until just cooked, turning the potatoes over halfway through cooking. Wrap in a clean cloth to keep warm. Set aside.

2. While the potatoes are cooking, peel and finely chop the onion. Combine with the oil in a small bowl. Cover and cook on Full Power for 3 minutes or until soft.

3. Add all the other ingredients except the potatoes. Mix thoroughly and cook on Full Power for 10 minutes, stirring occasionally until thick. Purée in the liquidizer or blender, adding 2 tablespoons water.

4. Without peeling, slice the potatoes thickly and arrange in a shallow dish. Pour the puréed sauce over. Cover the dish and cook on Full Power for 5 minutes until hot. Give the dish a half-turn halfway through cooking. Garnish with curry leaves.

Note: This will freeze but the texture will be more floury. It is suitable for vegans.

ROSEMARY SCENTED MUSHROOMS

Serves 4

Imperial (Metric):
1 lb (455g) button mushrooms, quartered

93

1 tablespoon sunflower oil
½ oz (15g) skimmed milk powder
3 tablespoons wholemeal flour
Sea salt
Freshly milled black pepper
½ teaspoon dried rosemary leaves
4 tablespoons medium white wine

1. Put the mushrooms into a large bowl, add the oil and toss until well coated. Cover and cook on Full Power for 5 minutes, stirring occasionally. Remove the mushrooms with a slotted spoon and set aside.

2. Whisk the milk powder and flour into the juices remaining in the bowl and season to taste with salt and pepper. Add the rosemary.

3. Cook uncovered on Full Power for 30 seconds, then whisk in the wine. Cook for a further 1-1½ minutes, whisking frequently, until the sauce thickens.

4. Return the mushrooms to the sauce and cook for 1 minute, stirring once during cooking. Stir again before serving.

Note: Do not freeze. Vegans may omit the milk powder.

SPICED COURGETTES

Serves 4

Imperial (Metric)
1 lb (455g) firm courgettes
¼ teaspoon ground coriander
¼ teaspoon ground cardamom
¼ teaspoon freshly milled black pepper
1 tablespoon white sesame seeds
2 tablespoons finely chopped cashew nuts
Sea salt

1. Rinse, top and tail the courgettes and cut into 2-inch (5cm) sticks.

2. Mix together the coriander, cardamom, pepper, seeds and nuts. Arrange layers of courgette in a small oval dish, sprinkling each layer with the spiced mixture.

3. Cover the dish and cook on Full Power for 3-3½ minutes. Leave to stand for 2 minutes before testing for tenderness. Add extra time if desired.

4. Season with salt and stir before serving, topped with a dab of butter if liked.

Note: Do not freeze this dish. It reheats quickly and well uncovered. It is suitable for vegans.

SPLIT PEAS IN COCONUT MILK

Serves 4

Imperial (Metric):
6 oz (170g) desiccated coconut
1¾ pint (1 litre) cold water
1 large onion,
1 clove garlic, crushed
2 dry chillis, chopped
1 teaspoon ground cumin
8 oz (225g) split peas
1 tablespoon lemon juice
1 teaspoon raw cane sugar
Sea salt
Freshly ground black pepper

1. Mix the coconut with ¾ pint (425ml) of water in a large bowl. Cook on Full Power for 5-7 minutes or until boiling. Cover tightly and leave for 30 minutes.

2. While the coconut is infusing, peel and finely slice the onion. Put with the garlic in a very large bowl. Cover and cook on Full Power, stirring occasionally, for 4 minutes until just beginning to brown.

3. Add the chillis and cumin and cook for a further minute.

4. Add the split peas and remaining water. Three-quarters cover and cook on Full Power for 15 minutes, stirring occasionally.

5. Strain the coconut liquid into the split peas. Reserve the coconut. Three-quarters cover and cook on Full Power for 5 minutes.

6. Reduce the setting to Defrost/Low and cook for 20 minutes. Remove the cover, raise the setting and cook on Full Power, stirring occasionally, until the split peas are soft and the mixture is still moist. Stir in the lemon juice and sugar. Set aside.

7. Spread the reserved coconut on a sheet of non-stick baking parchment. Place in the microwave and cook on Full Power for 13-15 minutes, stirring frequently until dry and beginning to brown.

8. Mix 2-3 tablespoons of the coconut into the split peas, then reheat on Full Power for 2-5 minutes, stirring once during cooking. Season with salt and pepper to taste.

9. Spoon into a serving dish and sprinkle with some of the remaining coconut. Reserve the surplus for use in other dishes.

Note: This freezes well. It is suitable for vegans.

STUFFED POTATOES

Serves 4

Imperial (Metric):
4×6 oz (170g) baking potatoes
1 large onion
2 oz (55g) butter or margarine

2 medium tomatoes
Sea salt
Freshly milled black pepper
2 oz (55g) grated cheese

1. Wash and dry the potatoes. Prick all over with a fork.

2. Arrange in a circle on a sheet of kitchen paper. Cook uncovered on Full Power for 10 minutes, turning each potato over after 6 minutes. Press to make sure that the potatoes are soft. Wrap in a clean cloth.

3. While the potatoes are cooking, peel and dice the onion. Put in a large bowl with the butter or margarine. Cover and cook on Full Power for 3 minutes, stirring occasionally, until soft.

4. Halve the tomatoes and de-seed if preferred. Dice the flesh and stir into the onions.

5. Cut the potatoes in half lengthwise scoop out the pulp with a teaspoon, then mash lightly and fold into the mixture. Season to taste with salt and pepper.

6. Pile the filling into the potato shell and arrange them in a circle in the microwave. Cook on Full Power for 2 minutes until heated through. Give each potato a half-turn after one minute.

7. Sprinkle cheese on top and brown under a preheated grill.

Note: Do not freeze. Vegans should substitute vegetable fat for butter and omit the cheese.

SWEDE AND CARROT PURÉE

Serves 4-6

Imperial (Metric):
1 lb (455g) swede
Approximately ¼-½ pint (140-285ml) water
8 oz (225g) cooked carrots
Sea salt
Freshly milled black pepper
4 tablespoons single cream

1. Wash the swede. Do not peel but remove and discard a slice from the bottom.

2. Place in a medium bowl and add water to reach 1-inch (2½cm) up the sides. Cover tightly and cook on Full Power for 10 minutes, turning the vegetable over halfway through cooking. Leave to stand for 5 minutes.

3. Carefully remove the swede, test with a sharp knife through the cut end to see if it is tender and return to the bowl and cook for a further 5 minutes if necessary. Do not throw the cooking water away until you are satisfied that the vegetable is cooked.

4. Put the swede on a board flat side down and, using a sharp knife and fork, remove the peel. Dice the flesh and purée in the blender with the carrots. Season to taste with salt and pepper, return to the bowl and cook on Full Power for 2-3 minutes until reheated. Stir in the cream.

Note: This freezes well without the cream, which means that it can be cooked and puréed at any convenient time, to be thawed and reheated on Full Power in about 5 minutes. Add the cream just before serving. It is not suitable for vegans unless the cream is omitted.

TOMATOES HALOUMI

Serves 4-8

Imperial (Metric):
4×8 oz (225g) Moroccan (beef) tomatoes
Sea salt
Freshly milled black pepper
Garlic Powder
4×¼-inch (½cm) slices Haloumi cheese halved
Mint leaves

1. Halve the tomatoes and put cut-side upwards in a shallow dish or on the oven shelf so they fit snugly.

2. Sprinkle the tomatoes with salt, pepper and a shake of garlic powder and cook uncovered on Full Power for 4 minutes. Reposition the tomatoes, placing those in the centre on the outside, giving each tomato a half turn. Cook for a further 2 minutes. A sign of cooking is when the pulp rises.

3. Top each tomato with Haloumi and a mint leaf and cook on Full Power for 5 minutes or until the tomatoes are tender but still holding their shape. Serve hot.

Note: Do not freeze. This is *not* suitable for vegans.

TURBAN OF CAULIFLOWER

Serves 4

Imperial (Metric):
4 tablespoons wholemeal flour
Sea salt
Freshly milled black pepper
1 small onion, peeled and cut into rings
1 oz (30g) polyunsaturated margarine
¾ pint (425ml) milk
1 lb (455g) cauliflower florets
1 oz (30g) flaked almonds

1. Mix 1 tablespoon of the flour with a little salt and pepper and toss in the onion rings, then shake off and reserve the surplus flour.

2. Put the margarine in a medium bowl and heat on Full Power for 20 seconds or until melted.

3. Add the onion and cook on Full Power for 4-5 minutes or until golden, turning the rings over once during cooking.

4. Stir in both the reserved seasoned flour and the unseasoned flour and add the milk. Stir thoroughly and cook on Full Power for 4-5 minutes, stirring occasionally with a whisk. Adjust the seasoning. Leave to stand, covered, while cooking the cauliflower.

5. Fill a small bowl with cauliflower florets interspersed with the almonds— arrange them so that the cauliflower shape is reconstructed in the base. Cover and cook on Full Power for 6 minutes or until only just tender.

6. Turn the cauliflower out on to a hot serving dish, reshaping the vegetable if necessary, and pour the onion sauce over.

Note: Brown under the grill if desired. Do not freeze. This is *not* suitable for vegans.

TYROLEAN RED CABBAGE

Serves 6-8

Imperial (Metric):
1 lb (455g) red cabbage, thick stem removed
1×6 oz cooking apple, cored
1 oz (30g) seedless raisins
¼ pint (140ml) salted water
4 tablespoons redcurrant jelly
1 tablespoon fresh lemon juice
¼ teaspoon freshly milled black pepper
1-3 tablespoons raw cane sugar

1. Finely shred the cabbage and put into a large casserole. Grate in the apple and add the raisins, salted water, redcurrant jelly, lemon juice, and pepper.

2. Cover with the lid and cook on Full Power for 15 minutes until the cabbage is just tender, stirring occasionally during cooking. Leave to stand, covered, for 5 minutes, then stir in the sugar to taste.

Note: This freezes well. It is suitable for vegans.

VEGETABLE PLATTER

Serves 6

Imperial (Metric):
8 oz (225g) carrots
Approximately ¼ pint (140ml) salted water
6 oz (170g) frozen or freshly cooked peas
2 large baking potatoes
6 oz (170g) courgettes
3 small tomatoes
2 tablespoons mayonnaise

1. Peel and slice the carrots. Place in an oval dish with half the water. Cover and cook on Full Power for 5-6 minutes until al dente. Drain and refresh under cold running water and drain again. Cover and set aside.

2. Cover and cook frozen peas with the remaining water in the same dish on Full Power for 4 minutes. Drain and refresh. Cover and set aside.

3. Wash and dry the potatoes. Prick with a fork, place on a piece of kitchen paper and cook on Full Power for 10-12 minutes, turning the potatoes over halfway through cooking. Do not overcook. Wrap in a clean cloth and set aside.

4. Wash and trim the courgettes and thinly slice.

5. Using the largest microwave suitable serving plate that will fit into your oven, arrange a circle of courgettes around the edge. Spread out the carrots in a border next to the courgettes and follow with a ring of peas.

6. Peel the cooked potatoes and cut into large dice and arrange in the middle of the plate.

7. Cut the tomatoes in half and make a space in the centre of the potatoes and place the tomatoes cut-side uppermost in this space.

8. Cover with kitchen paper and cook on Full Power for 4 minutes. Spoon on the mayonnaise, spreading slightly with the back of a spoon. Cook uncovered on Full Power for 4 minutes or until the vegetables are hot and the tomatoes are cooked.

Note: Do not freeze but the platter, which is delightful for a dinner party, can be assembled up to stage 7 to be cooked just before serving. Suitable for vegans if vinaigrette is substituted for mayonnaise.

PRESERVES AND SAUCES

Jams retain their colour and fruity flavour if made in small quantities. Long cooking after sugar is added discolours and darkens preserves. Make sure that the fruit is tender before adding the sugar. Soft berries take only 2 or 3 minutes and require no additional water. Blackcurrants and redcurrants, blueberries and cranberries should be cooked in a few tablespoons of water first until the skins soften.

Dessert sauces can just be puréed fruit or melted jam. You can add carob, puréed fruit or sweetening and flavouring to the basic white sauce, or prepare a simple sauce by thickening fruit juice with arrowroot. Blend 1 spoon of arrowroot with 2 tablespoons cold water, add to the juice and cook on Full Power, stirring occasionally, until the sauce has thickened.

Savoury sauces may be variations of the basic white or emulsified sauces, puréed vegetables or thickened stocks. To make a basic brown sauce, sauté chopped onions in a tablespoon of oil, then stir in flour and dark ingredients such as yeast extract and tomato purée. Flavour with good strong stock and fresh herbs and bring to the boil to thicken.

Most conventional recipes can be adapted for microwave cooking and the majority freeze successfully.

BÉARNAISE SAUCE

Serves 4

Imperial (Metric):
1 shallot, peeled and finely chopped
3¼ oz (92g) unsalted butter
3 tablespoons tarragon vinegar
Pinch sea salt
3 teaspoons chopped fresh chervil
2 egg yolks, beaten

1. Put the shallot and ¼ oz (7g) butter in a 1 pint (570ml) jug or bowl. Cover and cook on Full Power for 2 minutes until the shallot is soft. Shake the jug once during cooking to make sure the butter is thoroughly mixed in.

2. Add the vinegar, salt and 1 teaspoon chervil. Cook, uncovered, on Full Power for 3 minutes until the liquid is reduced to only 1 teaspoon.

3. Meanwhile, strain the egg yolks into a medium bowl (to remove the threads) and beat with an electric whisk until frothy (a hand beater will not produce good enough results).

4. Add the remaining 3 oz (85g) butter to the shallot and vinegar mixture. Cook, uncovered, on Full Power for 1 minute. Stir with a fork.

5. Cover and cook on Full Power for a further minute until bubbling. If you do not cover for the second minute, the butter will splatter.

6. As soon as the butter is bubbling, quickly remove the covering and whisk the egg yolks vigorously whilst pouring the butter in a steady stream over the beater. Two hands are needed for this vital stage.

7. Fold in the remaining chervil.

Note: Surprisingly, microwave Béarnaise sauce freezes well. Defrost for about 2 minutes on the lowest setting, stirring frequently until soft but not liquid. It is *not* suitable for vegans.

BLACKCURRANT JAM

Makes 2 lb (900g)

Imperial (Metric):
1 lb (455g) blackcurrants or blueberries, frozen, or fresh, trimmed and rinsed
1 lb (455g) granulated raw cane sugar

1. Put the berries in a very large bowl. Add ¼ pint (140ml) water. Three-quarters cover and cook on Full Power for 10 minutes or until the skins are soft. Stir twice during cooking.

2. Stir in the sugar until dissolved. This should not take long since the liquid is hot.

3. Uncover and cook on Full Power for 15 minutes, stirring occasionally. Test for setting by placing a spoon of the hot liquid on to a cold plate. The syrup should wrinkle when pushed with the spoon handle. Add extra cooking time if necessary.

4. Pot in two hot sterilized jars. Cover in the usual way.

Note: Jam can be stored in the freezer but will not set because the sugar content is high. Keep in a cool place or in the refrigerator. It is suitable for vegans.

CARROT MARMALADE

Makes approximately 1 lb (455g)

Imperial (Metric):
8 oz (225g) carrots
1 lemon
1 orange
1 lb (455g) raw cane granulated sugar
2 fl oz (60ml) water

1. Peel and grate the carrots. Rinse and dry the lemon and orange and grate the rind. Squeeze the juice from one lemon. Peel the orange, removing all the pith, then segment and chop the flesh.

2. Mix together the grated carrot, grated rind, lemon juice, chopped orange, sugar, and water in a very large bowl.

3. Cook on Full Power for 2 minutes. Stir until all the sugar is completely dissolved.

4. Cook uncovered on Full Power for 5 minutes. Stir, then continue cooking for 10 minutes or until a little of the syrup placed on a chilled saucer wrinkles when pushed with a spoon handle.

5. Pot in the usual way.

Note: This may be stored in the refrigerator. It is suitable for vegans.

HOLLANDAISE SAUCE

The microwave method for making this sauce is much easier than the conventional method. You can make it with soft margarine instead of butter but unfortunately it is not suitable for vegans as eggs are an integral part.

For every 2 oz (55g) butter or margarine, use 1 egg yolk and 2 teaspoons fresh lemon juice, adding sea salt and freshly milled black pepper to taste.

1. Put the butter or margarine in a small bowl and heat on Full Power for 30 seconds or until melted and slightly liquified.

2. Beat the egg yolk and lemon juice together and strain into the melted fat.

3. Cook small quantities on Defrost/Low, beating every 20 seconds with a wire whisk until the sauce begins to thicken (about 1½ minutes). Season to taste with salt and pepper and beat vigorously until the sauce cools.

Note: Cook a double or larger quantity on Full Power, beating every 15 seconds. A double quantity takes only about 45 seconds.

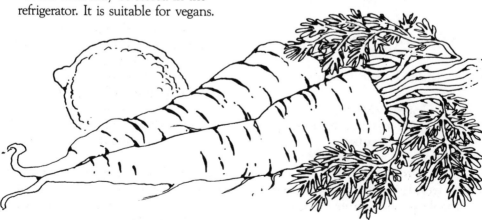

LEMON AND PARSLEY SAUCE

Makes ¼ pint (140ml)

Imperial (Metric):
1 small lemon
1 teaspoon arrowroot
2 tablespoons milk
4 oz (115g) soft low-fat cheese (quark)
1 teaspoon unrefined soft light brown sugar
2 tablespoons fresh parsley sprigs
Sea salt
Freshly milled black pepper

1. Cut the lemon in half. Squeeze the juice from one half and segment the remaining flesh.

2. Blend the arrowroot and milk in a small basin and cook on Full Power for 30 seconds or until boiling. Stir briskly to remove any lumps.

3. Purée the lemon juice, thickened milk, cheese, sugar and parsley sprigs in the liquidizer. Add the lemon segments and process briefly until finely chopped. Season with salt and pepper to taste.

Note: Do not freeze. This is *not* suitable for vegans.

MALTAISE SAUCE

Makes ¼ pint (140ml)

Imperial (Metric):
3 oz (85g) unsalted butter
2 egg yolks
Juice of 1 small orange
Pinch sea salt
Pinch freshly milled black pepper
2 tablespoons double cream

1. Put the butter in a small bowl and heat on Full Power for 30 seconds. Stir, then continue heating for 30 seconds or until the butter has melted but *not* separated.

2. Whisk together the egg yolks, orange juice and seasonings and strain into the melted butter. Stir in the cream.

3. Cook the sauce on Full Power for 30-45 seconds, whisking every 15 seconds, until the sauce thickens to the consistency of half-whipped cream.

4. Remove the bowl from the microwave and whisk until the sauce cools.

Note: Serve with courgettes, asparagus, artichoke bottoms, or young turnips. The sauce freezes well. Thaw and gently warm on the Defrost/Low setting, stirring briskly every 20 seconds. Polyunsaturated margarine can be used instead of the butter but the flavour and texture will not be as good. This is *not* suitable for vegans.

MARROW AND GINGER JAM

Makes 2 lb (900g)

Imperial (Metric):
3 lb (1.3kg) marrow
Grated rind and juice of 2 small lemons
¼ cooking apple
1½ tablespoons freshly grated ginger root
1½ lb (680g) raw cane granulated sugar

1. Trim and peel the marrow. Cut in half lengthwise and scoop out the pulp and seeds which can be retained to cook separately as a vegetable.

2. Roughly cut the marrow in ½-inch (1cm) chunks and put into a very large bowl with the lemon rind and juice, the apple finely chopped, and the grated ginger.

3. Cover the bowl tightly and cook on Full Power for 10 minutes or until tender, stirring once during cooking. Mash with a potato masher.

4. Stir the sugar into the stewed marrow and cook uncovered on Full Power for 5 minutes. Stir until all the sugar crystals have dissolved.

5. Remove the cover and cook for 25-30 minutes, stirring only if the mixture rises to the rim of the bowl. Test for setting by spooning a little of the syrup on to a chilled saucer. The jam is ready if the syrup wrinkles when pushed with the spoon handle.

6. Stir before spooning into hot sterilized jars. Seal in the usual way.

Note: This is suitable for vegans.

MELBA SAUCE

Makes 7 fl oz (200ml)

Imperial (Metric):
4 tablespoons redcurrant jelly (see below)
2 tablespoons clear honey
8 oz (225g) raspberries
2½ teaspoons arrowroot

1. Put the jelly and honey in a lipped bowl and heat on Full Power for 45 seconds or until the jelly is melted.

2. Stir in the raspberries and cook on Full Power for 4 minutes or until very soft. Crush, then press through a sieve to remove the seeds.

3. Blend the arrowroot with 2 tablespoons cold water. Stir into the purée and cook on Full Power for 1½-2 minutes or until thickened. Stir frequently during cooking. Cover and set aside until cool.

Note: Do not freeze. This is suitable for vegans provided honey is acceptable.

REDCURRANT JELLY

Makes 8 fl oz (225g)

Imperial (Metric):
1 lb (455g) redcurrants
Raw cane granulated sugar

1. Rinse, drain and pick over the currants, and put into a very large bowl. Crush with a potato masher.

2. Add ¼ pint (140ml) water. Cover and cook on Full Power for 6-7 minutes until the colour drains from the fruit. Crush once more. Line a nylon strainer with muslin and place over a large bowl. Pour in the redcurrant mixture and leave to drain overnight.

3. Measure the juice and add 8 oz (225g) sugar to every ½ pint (285ml) juice. Cook on Full Power for 2 minutes, then stir until the sugar is dissolved. Cook for 2 or 3 minutes or until boiling, then continue cooking until a spoonful of the syrup wrinkles when dropped on to a cold saucer and is pushed with the back of a spoon.

Note: Do not freeze. Stir in a covered container. This is suitable for vegans.

Soya and Sherry Sauce

Makes ¼ pint (140ml)

Imperial (Metric):
6 tablespoons water
2 tablespoons soya sauce
2 tablespoons sherry
¼ teaspoon freshly milled black pepper
1 teaspoon arrowroot

1. Combine all the ingredients in a 1 pint (570ml) jug. Cook on Full Power for 3 minutes or until the sauce thickens. Stir frequently during cooking.

Note: Do not freeze. This is suitable for vegans.

Tomato and Horseradish Sauce

Makes ½ pint (285ml)

Imperial (Metric):
1 tablespoon vegetable oil
1 onion, peeled and sliced
1 clove garlic, peeled
2-3 tablespoons grated horseradish
1 × 14 oz (395g) can tomatoes
1 vegetable stock cube
½ teaspoon Holbrook's sauce
Sea salt
Freshly milled black pepper

1. Mix the oil, onion and garlic in a medium bowl. Cover and vent with plastic film and cook on Full Power for 3 minutes to soften the onions.

2. Stir in the remaining ingredients except the salt and pepper. Cover and vent and cook on Full Power for 10 minutes, stirring once during cooking.

3. Purée in the liquidizer or blender. Pour back into the bowl. Season with salt and pepper and reheat on Full Power for 1-2 minutes. Stir before use.

Note: Serve with wholemeal pasta or nutmeat balls or poached eggs. Freezes well. It is suitable for vegans.

Tomato and Sage Sauce

Makes ⅛ pint (70ml)

Imperial (Metric):
2 oz (55g) unsalted butter
1 teaspoon fresh sage, finely snipped
2 tablespoons tomato purée
1 tablespoon water
1 egg, beaten
Sea salt
Freshly milled black pepper

1. Put the butter in a medium bowl and heat on Full Power for 30 seconds. Stir and heat for a further 30 seconds until melted.

2. Stir in the sage, tomato purée, water and lastly the egg.

3. Cook on Full Power for 30 seconds, then beat with a wire whisk. Cook for a further 30-45 seconds, beating every 15 seconds until the sauce thickens to the consistency of half-whipped cream. Do not overcook or the sauce will curdle.

4. Season to taste with salt and pepper and serve with pasta or nut roasts.

Note: The sauce freezes adequately and should be thawed on the Defrost/Low setting, beating frequently. It is *not* suitable for vegans.

VANILLA SAUCE

Makes ¾ pint (425ml)

Imperial (Metric):
**¾ pint (425ml) milk
½ teaspoon vanilla essence
1½ tablespoons cornflour
2 oz (55g) raw cane granulated sugar
2 egg yolks**

1. Put the milk into a lipped bowl and stir in the vanilla essence, cornflour and sugar. Cook on Full Power for 2½ minutes. Stir and cook for a further 2½-3 minutes until the sauce thickens. Stir frequently during cooking.

2. Beat the egg yolks in a jug, then add 3 tablespoons of the hot sauce. Beat thoroughly, then strain into the sauce. Mix well.

3. Reduce the setting to Defrost/Low and cook for a further 1-2 minutes, stirring occasionally, or until the sauce thickens sufficiently to coat the back of a spoon. Serve hot or cover with a damp disc of greaseproof paper until required.

Note: Do not freeze. This is *not* suitable for vegans.

VEGAN LOW-CALORIE SAUCE

Imperial (Metric):
**1×7 oz (200g) can tomatoes
2 spring onions, trimmed and finely sliced
¼ teaspoon bayleaf powder
Sea salt
Freshly milled black pepper
1 teaspoon cornflour**

1. Drain the tomatoes, reserving the juice.

2. Put the tomatoes into a small bowl and add the onions. Cook on Full Power for 8 minutes, stirring occasionally. Add the bayleaf powder and salt and pepper to taste.

3. Blend the cornflour with the reserved juice, stir into the cooked tomatoes and cook for a further 2-3 minutes, stirring occasionally, until the sauce thickens.

Note: Freezes adequately but beat thoroughly and add a little tomato juice when thawing and reheating.

PUDDINGS, CAKES AND DESSERTS

A steamed pudding or cake in five minutes is a reality in the microwave, so you will find yourself making them more often.

The selection of recipes in this section have been specially devised for the microwave. It is not advisable to adapt conventional recipes unless you are prepared to have a few failures. The microwave will not brown, so dark coloured ingredients are essential.

The cooking and rising process is totally different in the microwave. Conventionally baked cakes rise and stay up. In the microwave you must use dishes that are at least one-third taller than the expected height of the cooked cake or pudding. Mixtures which rise above the rim of the dishes will simply overspill as there is no hot air to create a crust.

The crust on conventional cakes prevents them from going stale too quickly because it holds in the moisture. Microwaved cakes (except when iced) and steamed puddings, on the other hand, must be wrapped in foil or cling-film while they are very fresh.

Cake and pudding batters should be slightly wetter when microwaving. Turn the dishes during cooking if the mixture seems to be rising unevenly and cook only until just dry on top. Give a standing time of at least 5 or preferably 10 minutes to ensure the underneath is properly cooked.

A base lining of non-stick baking parchment prevents baked goods from sticking.

Stew fruit in deep bowls or casseroles, using a minimum of extra liquid, and stir occasionally to prevent overspill. Crumble toppings can be sprinkled over the fruit before cooking but the boil-over risk is lessened if they are added when the fruit is tender.

Cook egg custards on the Defrost/Low setting to prevent curdling.

Gelatine is not acceptable to the vegetarian and agar agar or gelozone must be substituted. Converts will notice a difference in the type of gelling, which never becomes rubbery. I have found it better to add agar agar to cold liquid and then bring it to the boil, rather than using the traditionally accepted sprinkle on the hot liquid method.

When using raw cane sugar for syrup-making, bear in mind that the colour will appear darker, even at the beginning of the cooking period, but this does not mean that the syrup will cook more quickly. Test syrups with a sugar thermometer or by spooning a few drops into cold water in the usual way.

APPLE BASKETS

Serves 4

Imperial (Metric):
4 red dessert apples
Few drops vegetable oil
1-2 tablespoons fresh lemon juice
4 celery stalks
2 oz (55g) walnuts, refreshed (see page 29) and coarsely chopped
4 fresh dates, skinned and sliced
4 oz (115g) cottage cheese

1. Wash and dry the apples. To give them a shine, rub them with kitchen paper sprinkled with a drop of vegetable oil.

2. Cut off a slice from the stalk end of the apples and, using a grapefruit knife, carefully remove the whole of the inside, making certain you do not break through the skins. Remove the cores and chop the flesh.

3. Brush the inside walls of the apples with lemon juice and mix the remaining juice and chopped apple together.

4. Finely chop three of the celery stalks and mix with the chopped apple. Cut the remaining stalk lengthwise into four pieces. Put into a small dish, just cover with water and cover and cook on Full Power for 2-3 minutes to blanch. Drain and plunge into cold water until cool. Drain again and dry.

5. Mix the apples, chopped celery, walnuts, dates and cheese together. Pile into the apple shells. Insert a blanched celery strip into one side of the apple mixture and curve over to form a handle, pressing the tip into the opposite side.

Note: Do not freeze. These are *not* suitable for vegans unless tofu is substituted for the cheese.

APPLE SNOW

Serves 4

Imperial (Metric):
1 lb (455g) dessert apples, peeled, cored and sliced
1 teaspoon finely grated lemon zest
2 drops almond essence
2 egg whites
2 oz (55g) raw cane granulated sugar
1 tablespoon flaked almonds

1. Put the apple, lemon zest and almond essence in a medium bowl, cover tightly and cook on Full Power for 4-5 minutes until pulpy.

2. Purée in the liquidizer or blender and leave to cool.

3. Whisk the egg whites until soft peaks form, then gradually whisk in the sugar. Fold half the mixture into the apple purée. Half-fill four microwave suitable sundae dishes with the purée and pile the meringue on top.

4. Arrange the dishes in a circle in the microwave and cook uncovered on Full Power for 1½-2 minutes until the meringue is puffy and mallow-like.

5. Sprinkle flaked almonds on top of the meringue and quickly brown at a 6-inch (15cm) distance from a hot grill. This takes only 5 seconds.

Note: Only the apple pulp can be frozen. Complete the recipe after thawing. This is *not* suitable for vegans.

BAKED APPLE COCKTAIL

Serves 4

Imperial (Metric):
**4×6 oz (170g) cooking apples
7.8 oz (225g) can fruit cocktail in natural juice
1 teaspoon arrowroot
1 teaspoon cold water**

1. Wash and core the apples and score with a sharp knife at four equidistant places from top to bottom. Put in a shallow dish.

2. Strain the juice from the fruit cocktail over the apples. Cover and cook on Full Power for 3-4 minutes or until soft, turning each apple round once during cooking.

3. Remove the apples to a serving dish and keep warm.

4. Blend the arrowroot and water together and stir into the fruit juices. Cook on Full Power for 40 seconds-1 minute, stirring once during cooking.

5. Stir in the fruit and cook on Full Power for a further minute, stirring once, until the juice has thickened and the fruit is warm.

6. Stuff a little of the fruit into the centre of each apple and pour the remainder over. Serve hot.

Note: Do not freeze as this collapses the apples. This dish is suitable for vegans.

BAKED JACKET BANANAS IN ORANGE WITH MAPLE SAUCE

Serves 4

Imperial (Metric):
**¼ pint (140ml) natural yogurt
1 tablespoon maple syrup
1 large orange
4 medium bananas**

1. To make the sauce, blend the yogurt and syrup together.

2. Wash and dry the orange, pare thin strips of the rind and shred finely.

3. Put the orange shreds into a jug, cover with cold water and cook on Full Power for 2 minutes or until tender. Drain and set aside.

4. Halve the orange. Squeeze the juice from one half, and segment and chop the other.

5. Rinse and dry the bananas and place them, unpeeled, in an oval or rectangular dish. Slash the tops lengthwise.

6. Pour the orange juice on to the banana flesh through the slash and cook on Full Power for 2 minutes. Reposition the bananas, placing those in the centre on the outside. Top with the orange segments, reduce the setting to Defrost/Low and cook for 4½-5 minutes. Garnish with the reserved orange strips.

7. Serve hot with the maple yogurt sauce.

Note: Do not freeze. This is suitable for vegans provided the sauce is omitted.

BUDUM DADH

Serves 6

Imperial (Metric):
**1×6 oz (170g) can evaporated milk
14 fl oz (395ml) boiling water
4 oz (115g) ground almonds
2 drops natural almond essence
1 oz (30g) muscovado sugar
½ oz (15g) chopped skinned
pistachio nuts**

1. In a large bowl mix together the evaporated milk and the water. Stir in the ground almonds, almond essence and sugar.

2. Cook on Full Power for 5 minutes. Stir thoroughly and reduce the setting to Defrost/Low and continue cooking, stirring occasionally for 30 minutes or until the mixture is the consistency of thick custard.

3. Pour into individual glasses, sprinkle with the chopped pistachios and serve hot or cold with boudoir or wafer biscuits.

Note: Do not freeze but this rich sweet Indian dessert will keep in the refrigerator for a few days. It is *not* suitable for vegans.

CHILLED SOUFFLÉ GRAND MARNIER

Serves 6

Imperial (Metric):
**2 eggs
1½ oz (45g) granulated raw cane
sugar
7 fl oz (200ml) double cream
2 teaspoons Grand Marnier
1 teaspoon grated orange rind**

1. Cut six long strips of greaseproof paper to the height of the individual ramekin dishes, plus 1 inch (2½cm). Wrap around the dishes, fixing with rubber bands. A well-shaped paper collar will ensure a realistic soufflé appearance.

2. Put the eggs and sugar in a medium bowl, and beat with an electric whisk until light and frothy. Cook on Defrost/Low for 2-2½ minutes until thick and creamy. It is essential to whisk every 30 seconds.

3. Whip the cream and Grand Marnier until soft peaks form. Carefully fold the cream into the egg mixture. Pour into the prepared dishes so that the mixture reaches well above the rims. The collar will prevent any overflow.

4. Open-freeze the dishes for at least 2 hours then cover and freeze until required.

5. Remove the ice cream from the freezer 15 minutes before serving, remove the rubber bands, then slide the warm blade of a table knife between the paper and the rim of the dish.

6. Decorate with orange rind and serve with wafer biscuits.

Note: This is *not* suitable for vegans.

CHOCOLATE AND ORANGE JELLY CAKE

Serves 4-6

Imperial (Metric):
1 teaspoon agar agar
¾ pint (425ml) fresh orange juice
2-3 tablespoons raw cane granulated sugar
1 teaspoon ground ginger
3 oz (85g) dark dessert chocolate
Few drops vegetable oil
Pared rind of 1 orange

1. Sprinkle the agar agar on to the cold orange juice and stir in the sugar. Heat on Full Power for 2 minutes or until boiling. Stir in the ginger.

2. Pour the liquid into a 1 pint (570ml) jelly mould and leave to set. Unmould on to a serving dish.

3. Break up the chocolate and put into a large glass measuring jug. Heat on Full Power for 1-2 minutes until the surface of the chocolate glistens. Stir in the oil. Continue melting for a further 20 seconds if necessary.

4. Pour the melted chocolate over the jelly and leave until the chocolate is nearly set.

5. Remove all the white pith and cut the orange rind into thin strips. Put in a small bowl and just cover with water. Cook on Full Power for 3-4 minutes or until the strips are tender. Stir occasionally during cooking to prevent boiling over. Drain, cool and dry the strips on kitchen paper then arrange in a sunray pattern on the cake. Leave until the chocolate is set before serving.

Note: Do not freeze. This is suitable for vegans who are prepared to eat dark chocolate.

CHOCOLATE CAROB ROULADE

Serves 4

Imperial (Metric):
3 eggs, separated
3 oz (85g) raw cane granulated sugar
1 oz (30g) wholemeal flour
1 oz (30g) carob powder, sifted
1 tablespoon potato flour
1 tablespoon hot water
¼-½ pint (140-285ml) double cream, whipped
Granulated raw cane sugar to decorate

1. Shape a large sheet of non-stick vegetable parchment to make a deep rectangular tray approximately 10 inches×6 inches (25cm×15cm).

2. Whisk the egg yolks until frothy. Add the sugar and whisk again until thick. The mixture should leave a trail when a fork is drawn through the surface of the mixture.

3. Fold in the flour, carob and potato flour and add the water.

4. With clean beaters, whisk the egg whites until soft peaks form. Stir 1 tablespoon of the beaten whites into the cake mixture, then fold in the remainder with a metal tablespoon.

5. Pour the mixture into the parchment case and carefully place in the microwave. You may need to use two fish slices for this. Cook, uncovered, on Full Power for 3-4 minutes until the mixture is dry on top but still slightly sticky around the edges. If the sides of the tray

start to collapse during cooking, open the microwave door and coax them back into shape.

6. Allow to cool for about 5 minutes.

7. Open out the parchment border from the sides of the cake. With a table knife, mark the cake about ½ inch (1cm) from one short end. Place a rectangular piece of non-stick baking parchment on top of the cake and roll up like a Swiss roll with the parchment on both sides. Allow to cool completely.

8. When the cake is cold, carefully unroll, removing the parchment lining. Spread the inside with the cream, then re-roll without undue pressure which would force out the cream.

9. Lightly dust the outside of the cake with sugar.

Note: The undecorated cake can be frozen. It is *not* suitable for vegans.

CHOCOLATE DESSERT

Serves 4

Imperial (Metric):
1 oz (30g) carob powder, sifted
2 tablespoons cornflour
½ teaspoon vanilla essence
1 pint (570ml) milk
1 oz (30g) raw cane granulated sugar
½ oz (15g) butter or margarine

1. Mix the carob cornflour and vanilla essence with a little of the cold milk in a medium bowl.

2. Whisk in the remaining milk and cook on Full Power, whisking frequently, for 5 minutes until thickened. Stir in the sugar until dissolved.

3. Add the butter and cook for a further 30 seconds. Stir.

4. Divide the mixture between four individual dishes and leave to cool for 10 minutes, then cover the dishes and refrigerate until cold.

Note: Do not freeze. This is *not* suitable for vegans.

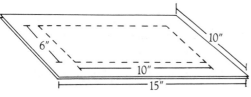

1. Take two sheets of non-stick vegetable parchment — 15×10 inches (38×25cm), laid on top of each other. Mark central box in pencil — 10×6 inches (25×10cm).

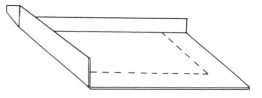

2. Fold along pencil lines (shown as dotted in the diagram) so sides stand vertically.

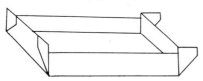

3. Mitre corners and fold outwards along shorter sides.

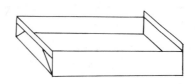

4. Fold higher edges over to the height of other edges — this will hold corners in place.

DATE AND APPLE CAKE

Makes 1 small loaf cake

Imperial (Metric):
2 tablespoons vegetable oil
2 eggs
3 tablespoons soft dark brown raw
cane sugar
½ teaspoon vanilla essence
1 tablespoon molasses
4 oz (115g) plain wholemeal flour
1 teaspoon baking powder
1 dessert apple, peeled, cored and
finely chopped
1 oz (30g) chopped dates

1. Lightly oil a 1½-pint (850ml) loaf dish and line the base with a non-stick vegetable parchment.

2. Beat together the eggs, sugar and vanilla essence until thick.

3. Stir in the oil and molasses.

4. Add the flour and baking powder. Mix well.

5. Mix the apple and dates into the batter.

6. Pour the mixture into the prepared dish and cook on Defrost/Low for 7 minutes or until just dry on top.

7. Leave the cake to stand in the dish for 5 minutes before turning out. Remove the parchment and reverse the cake on to a serving dish. Serve warm or leave to cool on a wire rack before wrapping in cling-film.

Note: This freezes well. It is *not* suitable for vegans.

EARLY RHUBARB CRUNCH

Serves 4-6

Imperial (Metric):
6 oz (170g) strawberries, halved and
rinsed
1 lb (450g) young rhubarb, cut into
1-inch (2½cm) lengths
¼ teaspoon ground ginger
1 × 10½ oz (298g) can mandarin
orange segments in natural juice
Raw can granulated sugar to taste
2 tablespoons low-fat natural yogurt
2-3 tablespoons crunchy muesli

1. Reserve four strawberries for decoration and slice the remainder.

2. Put the rhubarb in a large bowl, add the ground ginger and strained juice from the mandarin oranges. Cover and cook on Full Power for 10-12 minutes, stirring twice during cooking, until the rhubarb has pulped. Add sugar to taste.

3. Leave to cool, then stir in the yogurt and fold in the orange segments and sliced strawberries.

4. Spoon the mixture into individual glasses. Just before serving, sprinkle with the muesli and top with a strawberry.

Note: Do not freeze. Vegans should omit the yogurt.

FRUIT CRUMBLE

Serves 4-6

(Use any fruit that stews well, such as rhubarb, plums, redcurrants and gooseberries.)

Imperial (Metric):
**1½ lb (680g) prepared fruit
2 oz (55g) or more soft dark muscavado sugar to taste
½ teaspoon ground mixed spice**

Crumble topping:
**5 oz (140g) wholemeal or granary flour
1 oz (30g) rye flakes
½ oz (15g) millet flakes
2 tablespoons sesame seeds
4 oz (115g) soft margarine
2 oz (55g) soft dark muscavado sugar**

1. Put the fruit in a large deep dish, cover and cook on Full Power for 5 minutes or until hot. Stir once during cooking. (If using frozen fruit, add an extra 5 minutes cooking time.)

2. Stir the sugar and spice into the fruit. Cover and leave to stand while preparing the topping. This will help to dissolve the sugar.

3. Put the flour, flakes, margarine and sesame seeds into a mixing bowl or the food processor and blend together until pea-sized moist crumbs form. Mix in the well-crushed sugar.

4. Stir the fruit, then spoon on the topping and smooth the surface. Without covering, cook on Full Power for 8-12 minutes or until the topping is firm but not crisp. Leave to stand for 5 minutes, during which time the topping will crispen.

Note: Fruit tends to rise up the sides of the dish and the topping will undulate during cooking. This is suitable for freezing. Thaw on Full Power and reheat on the Defrost/Low setting. It is suitable for vegans if non-dairy margarine is substituted.

FUDGE BARS

Makes 16

Imperial (Metric):

Base:
**4 oz (115g) polyunsaturated
margarine
1 oz (30g) raw cane granulated sugar
1 egg yolk
4 oz (115g) wholemeal flour
2 oz (55g) porridge oats
3 tablespoons milk**

Filling:
**2 oz (55g) polyunsaturated margarine
2 oz (55g) raw cane granulated sugar
1 teaspoon honey
3 fl oz (85ml) condensed milk**

Topping:
**3 oz (85g) milk chocolate cake
covering**

1. Mix all the ingredients for the base in a bowl to form a soft dough.

2. Turn out on to a sheet of non-stick baking parchment and shape to a 6-inch (15cm) square. Chill.

3. Place the base on the parchment in the microwave and cook on Full Power for 3 minutes, turning the parchment four times during cooking. Lift on to a cooling wire and slide out the parchment.

4. To make the filling, put all the ingredients in a bowl. Cook on Full Power for 4 minutes or until light-brown and thick. Beat well every 30 seconds during cooking.

5. Pour the filling over the biscuit base and leave to cool.

6. Break the chocolate cake covering into small pieces and put in a jug. Cook on

Full Power for 1 minute. Stir and cook for a further 30 seconds if necessary until the chocolate is shiny. Stir until melted.

7. Spread the melted chocolate over the fudge. Leave to cool.

8. Cut into sixteen squares or bars with a warm knife.

Note: Store in an airtight container. Freeze if desired but thaw only at room temperature. This is *not* suitable for vegans.

GINGER CUP CAKES

Makes 12

Imperial (Metric):
**1 tablespoon molasses
1 tablespoon clear honey
2 tablespoons sunflower oil
1 tablespoon milk
1 oz (30g) rich dark molasses sugar
2 oz (55g) wholemeal flour
1/8 teaspoon bicarbonate of soda
2 teaspoons ground ginger
1 egg
24 small paper cake cases**

Icing:
**2 oz (55g) polyunsaturated margarine
4 tablespoons carob powder
1 oz (30g) icing sugar
2 oz (55g) chopped crystallized ginger**

1. Prepare twelve double-thickness paper cases.

2. Put the molasses, honey, oil, milk and sugar into a large bowl and beat thoroughly with a wire whisk. Cook on Full Power for 1 minute, stirring once during cooking. Beat until the sugar has completely dissolved.

3. Add the flour, bicarbonate of soda and ground ginger, then beat in the egg.

4. Half-fill the prepared cases with the cake batter and, using a fish slice to prevent them from spilling, transfer six to the microwave. Arrange them in a circle and cook on Full Power for 45 seconds-1 minute until the cakes are risen and only just dry on top. Cook the remaining six cakes in the same way.

To make the icing:

1. Put the margarine in a medium bowl and heat for 30 seconds or until melted.

2. Sift the carob and icing sugar into the melted margarine and add 1 tablespoon boiling water. Stir gently until the clouds of carob and sugar settle and the mixture is smooth.

3. Spread the icing over the warm cakes and decorate with chopped ginger. Leave until cool, then remove and discard the outer paper cases.

Note: Although icing sugar is not unrefined, I have used it because raw sugar is not successful in this type of icing. The cakes may be frozen without icing and allowed to thaw at room temperature. They are *not* suitable for vegans.

JACKO'S JUNKET

Serves 4

Imperial (Metric):
1 pint (570ml) milk
2 tablespoons carob powder
1 tablespoon raw cane granulated sugar
1 teaspoon grated orange rind
1 teaspoon vegetable rennet

1. Put the milk, carob, sugar and rind in a large bowl, stir and, without covering, heat on Full Power for 2 minutes or until the temperature reaches blood heat and feels warm to the touch.

2. Stir in the rennet and leave in a cool place, but *not* in the refrigerator, until set. Serve cold.

Note: Junket separates on standing, and if refrigerated, the amount of whey increases. Although acceptable it becomes unattractive. Do not freeze. This is *not* suitable for vegans.

JAMAICA ORANGES

Serves 4

Imperial (Metric):
2 large oranges
**2 tablespoons raw cane granulated
sugar**
1 teaspoon rum
1 small dessert apple
1 slice fresh or canned pineapple
1 banana
1 tablespoon chopped pistachio nuts

1. Halve the oranges and put in a
shallow dish, cut side down. Cook on
Full Power for 2 minutes until the juice
can be easily squeezed.

2. Gently squeeze the orange juice into a
bowl and scrape out the membranes. Set
the shells aside.

3. Stir the sugar into the orange juice
and cook on Full Power for 1-1½ minutes
until boiling. Stir, then cook for a
further 2 minutes or until a thin syrup is
formed. Add the rum.

4. Core and cube the apple, cut the
pineapple into wedges and peel and slice
the banana, mixing all the fruit into the
syrup. Cook on Full Power for 30
seconds, stir and cook for a further 30
seconds. Spoon the fruit into the orange
shells and pour the syrup over.

Note: Decorate with pistachio nuts. Do
not freeze this dish. It is suitable for
vegans.

MALTED BREAD AND BUTTER PUDDING

Serves 4

Imperial (Metric):
6 slices toasted malt fruit loaf
Butter or margarine
2 oz (55g) sultanas
2 oz (55g) currants
2 oz (55g) chopped mixed peel
½ pint (285ml) milk
2 eggs
½ teaspoon cinnamon

1. Butter the toast on one side. Cut
slices in half diagonally.

2. Place four pieces of toast, buttered side
down, in a 1½-pint dish (850ml) oval pie
dish. Sprinkle with a mixture of one-
third of the dried fruit. Cover with a
layer of toast, buttered side uppermost,
cover with half the remaining fruit.
Top with the remaining toast and fruit.

3. Put the milk into a large jug or
medium bowl and heat on Full Power for
1½-2 minutes until warm to the touch.
Beat in the eggs and cinnamon.

4. Pour the milky liquid into the dish of
toast and fruit. Reduce the setting to
Defrost/Low, cover with greased
greaseproof paper and cook for 20
minutes or until the custard is set
around the edges and beginning to set in
the middle. Raise the setting to Full
Power and cook for 1-2 minutes if the
middle is still runny. Leave to stand for
at least 5 minutes before serving.

Note: Do not freeze. This is *not* suitable
for vegans.

MALT FRUIT LOAF

Makes 2 loaves

Imperial (Metric):
3 oz (85g) malt extract
2 tablespoons molasses
3 tablespoons vegetable oil
1 lb (455g) wholemeal flour
¼ teaspoon sea salt
1 sachet easy-blend powder yeast
8 oz (225g) sultanas
6 fl oz (170ml) warm water

1. Combine the malt extract, molasses and oil and heat on Full Power for 30 seconds to soften and blend.

2. Mix the flour and salt together in a large bowl and heat on Full Power for 3 minutes, stirring occasionally to warm the flour. Stir in the yeast and sultanas.

3. Pour the liquid into the flour, add water and mix and knead. Divide into two loaf shapes.

4. Lightly oil two 1½-pint (850ml) loaf dishes and base line with non-stick vegetable parchment. Press in the shaped dough. Cover and leave to rise until doubled in size. Occasionally give 1 minute on 10% to speed the rising process.

5. When the dough has risen, cook the bases separately uncovered on Full Power for 3 minutes. Reduce the setting to Defrost/Low and cook for a further 5-6 minutes until the dough has set.

6. Leave for 5 minutes before turning out. Serve warm. The loaf becomes hard when cold but can be reheated whole or sliced. Do not overheat or the fruit will burn the mouth.

Note: This freezes for a week or two but it must be warmed before serving. It is suitable for vegans.

Marmalade Fruit Pudding

Serves 4

Imperial (Metric):
1 oz (30g) dried apricots
4 oz (115g) white vegetable fat
4 oz (115g) unrefined dark brown sugar
5 tablespoons marmalade
5 glacé cherries, quartered
Grated lemon rind
2 oz (55g) sultanas
1 oz (30g) ground rice
1 oz (30g) wholemeal flour
1 teaspoon baking powder
2 large eggs, beaten
4 oz (115g) malted brown granary breadcrumbs
1 tablespoon milk

1. Put the apricots in a jug just covered with water and heat on Full Power for 1 minute after the water has boiled (about 1 minute). Leave to stand for 10 minutes, then drain and chop.

2. Meanwhile, lightly oil a 2-pint (1.1-litre) bowl and place a small circle of non-stick vegetable parchment in the base.

3. Put the vegetable fat in a large bowl and heat on Full Power for 1-1½ minutes until melted.

4. Add the sugar and beat until it is thoroughly blended. Mix in the marmalade.

5. Add the cherries, grated lemon rind, apricots and sultanas. Mix the ground rice, flour and baking powder together and stir into the mixture.

6. Beat in the eggs and then add the breadcrumbs, stirring until they are fully incorporated. Add the milk to form a heavy batter.

7. Cook the pudding on Full Power for 5 minutes or until just dry on top. Cover and leave to stand for 8 minutes before turning out on to a suitable serving dish. Remove the parchment disc. If the pudding is still not set, return it, on the serving dish, to the microwave and cook on Full Power for a further 2 minutes.

Note: The pudding freezes well. Thaw and reheat covered on the Defrost/Low setting. It is *not* suitable for vegans.

Non-Dairy Carob and Pistachio Pudding with Apricot Sauce

Serves 4

Imperial (Metric):
8 oz (225g) firm tofu, drained
1 oz (30g) carob powder
2 tablespoons chopped pistachio nuts
4 oz (115g) raw cane granulated sugar

Apricot sauce:
1×8 oz (225g) can apricots in natural juice
1 teaspoon arrowroot

1. Mash the tofu to a smooth consistency in a food processor. Add the carob and most of the nuts. Continue processing until the nuts are coarsely chopped.

2. Stir the sugar into 2 tablespoons of water in a glass measuring jug. Cook on Full Power for 1 minute to dissolve the

sugar. Stir well. Continue cooking for a further minute or until boiling. Cook for 1 minute more until a syrup forms.

3. Stir the syrup into the carob mixture. Spoon into a small pie dish. Cook on Full Power for 1 minute. Sprinkle with the reserved nuts and leave to cool. Refrigerate for 2 or 3 hours until well chilled.

4. To make the sauce, purée the apricots and the juice with the arrowroot. Pour into a jug or bowl and cook on Full Power for 2-3 minutes, stirring occasionally, until thickened.

5. Cut the pudding into wedges and serve with the sauce.

Note: Do not freeze. This is suitable for vegans.

PRALINE ICE CREAM

Imperial (Metric):

Praline:
2 oz (55g) unblanched almonds
4 oz (115g) raw cane granulated sugar

Ice Cream:
½ pint (285ml) milk
4 oz (115g) raw cane granulated sugar
4 eggs
Few drops natural vanilla essence
¼ pint (140ml) double cream

1. Mix the almonds and sugar together on a large double sheet of non-stick baking parchment. Place in the microwave and cook on Full Power for approximately 6-10 minutes, stirring frequently with a wooden spoon until the sugar is melted and a brown syrup forms. Leave until hard (about 20 minutes).

2. Break up this almond brittle and grind or pound to a coarse powder.

3. In a large bowl, mix together the milk and sugar. Cook on Full Power for 1½-2 minutes until warm but not steaming.

4. Beat together the eggs and vanilla essence, add to the milk and whisk well.

5. Cook on Full Power for 1 minute. Whisk. Cook for a further 2 minutes, whisking frequently until slightly thickened. Cover and leave until cold. Do not overcook or the mixture will curdle.

6. Fold 2 tablespoons of the praline and all the cream into the cold sauce. Freeze until just beginning to firm. Beat vigorously and spoon into a mould, then cover and freeze until hard.

7. Transfer to room temperature for 15-30 minutes before serving, in order to slightly soften.

Note: The times given for cooking the praline can only be used as a guide. Caramelization may be quicker or considerably longer than stated. It is therefore important not to leave the mixture to cook unattended. Praline keeps well in an airtight container and can be used as topping on all creamy-type desserts.
It is *not* suitable for vegans.

RASPBERRY JELLY

Serves 4

Imperial (Metric):
**1 lb (455g) frozen or fresh
raspberries
8 fl oz (225ml) orange juice
(approximately)
2 tablespoons golden granulated raw
cane sugar
1 teaspoon agar agar
Whipped cream for decoration**

1. Put the raspberries into a large bowl. Cook on Full Power for 4-6 minutes until the juice runs freely.

2. Strain the juice from the raspberries into a measuring jug. Make up to ½ pint (285ml) with orange juice.

3. Stir the sugar and agar agar into the juice. Cook on Full Power for 2½ minutes or until boiling. Stir until dissolved, then leave to cool slightly.

4. Divide the raspberries between four serving dishes. Pour the juice over the fruit. Leave to set. Decorate with a large rosette of whipped cream.

Note: Do not freeze. This is suitable for vegans without the cream topping.

THICK YOGURT

Makes approximately 1 pint
(570ml)

Imperial (Metric):
**¾ pints (425ml) long life milk
4 tablespoons skimmed milk powder
4 tablespoons low-fat natural yogurt**

1. Put the milk in a large bowl and cook on Full power for 2 minutes. Stir and cook for a further 2-3 minutes until the milk boils.

2. Reduce the setting to Defrost/Low and cook for 8 minutes, stirring occasionally, until the milk is slightly reduced.

3. Whisk in the milk powder and leave to cool until comfortable to touch.

4. Whisk the yogurt into the milk, then pour into a wide-necked flask or divide between the sterilized jars in a yogurt-maker.

5. Cover with the lid(s) and leave for 8 hours until the yogurt is just set, then refrigerate, covered, for a further 3-4 hours.

Note: It is important to sterilize the jars or a satisfactory set may not occur. Do not freeze. When using home-made yogurt in cooking, add a teaspoon of cornflour. This is *not* suitable for vegans.

TIPSY BERRIES

Serves 4-6

Imperial (Metric):
**3 tablespoons raw cane granulated
sugar
8 fl oz (225ml) sweet red wine
2 tablespoons brandy
1 lb (455g) raspberries
4 oz (115g) blackcurrants
4 oz (115g) redcurrants**

1. Put the sugar and wine in a medium bowl and cook on Full Power for 2 minutes, stirring occasionally. Stir until the sugar is dissolved.

2. Cook for a further 5 minutes to form a light syrup, then mix in the brandy.

3. Rinse the fruit and trim if necessary. Put it into a serving bowl, then pour the syrup over. Chill thoroughly in the refrigerator, stirring occasionally.

Note: Do not freeze. The fruit flavour improves if the dish is left to stand for 24 hours. This is suitable for vegans.

WALNUT BROWNIES

Makes 16

Imperial (Metric):
6 oz (170g) polyunsaturated margarine
Few drops natural vanilla essence
6 oz (170g) raw cane sugar
3 oz (85g) wholemeal flour
3 eggs, beaten
2 oz (55g) carob powder
¼ teaspoon baking powder
¼ teaspoon salt
3 oz (85g) walnuts, coarsely chopped

1. Put the margarine in a large bowl and cook on Full Power for 1 minute until melted.

2. Thoroughly mix in the vanilla essence and sugar. Stir in 2 tablespoons of the flour, then add the egg a little at a time, beating vigorously.

3. Stir in the remaining flour and sift in the carob, baking powder and salt. Mix well. Fold in the walnuts.

4. Pour the mixture into a 6-inch×8½-inch (15cm×21cm) greased and base-lined shallow dish. Cook, uncovered, on Full Power for 4-5 minutes until just dry on top.

5. Leave to stand for 5 minutes, then loosen the edges with a knife and turn out on to a piece of non-stick baking parchment. Test in the middle and around the edges, and if not fully cooked, put the brownie block (still on the parchment) in the microwave and cook on Defrost/Low for a further 2-5 minutes. Do not overcook or the edges will become hard. Brownies set further on cooling.

6. While slightly warm, cut into 16-inch squares. When cool keep in an airtight tin.

Note: This freezes well. It is *not* suitable for vegans.

Some Menu Suggestions

Balancing the vegetarian diet is fairly simple. One of the major problems is the potential lack of the amino-acids which make up the proteins. Dairy fats are normally acceptable for non-vegans, though polyunsaturated fats are healthier. Carbohydrates are all suitable for vegetarians but non-refined sugar is better than refined, and wholemeal flour is better than white flour. Vegetarian foods are rich in fibre, which is an essential part of the healthy diet.

Protein in plants is divided into three categories:

1. Pulses, which include all the dried beans and peas, including lentils and peanuts.
2. Grains, including Bulgur, rice, wheat, corn, pasta, barley, and oats.
3. Seeds and nuts, including pumpkin, sunflower and sesame seeds, cashews, walnuts, pistachios, almonds, and hazelnuts.

In the animal protein group are the milk products such as cheese, yogurt, milk and butter. Vegetarians can also eat eggs, although they must obviously omit fish, meat and poultry.

When items in two or more of these groups are combined at one meal, the protein intake becomes complete. Rice with lentils, scrambled egg with chopped nuts, bread and cheese are a few examples of these mixes. Serve with fresh vegetables or fruit for a well balanced diet.

To make a menu interesting, a reasonable choice of foods must be offered. It is much more exciting to have a small portion of several items than one large serving of a single food. For this reason the number of servings indicated in each of the recipes can only be a guide. And appetites vary, of course. You will not need to cut down very much on the soups—a 7 fl oz (200ml) serving is average. The dessert servings are probably about right too. The main course items may need adjustment but most of the recipes will freeze or can be stored in the refrigerator for serving the next day—or you can invite a few people to supper.

Recipes Suitable for Vegans

Soups
Barley; Beetroot; Carrot; Green Lentil; Lettuce; Mulligatawny; Mushroom; Watercress; Vichyssoise.

Salads
Artichoke; Beetroot; Hot slaw; Kohlrabi; Planters; Russian; Spaghetti; Spinach; Tomato vegetable ring.

Main Courses
Almond apricotine stuffed pittas; Asparagus

mousse; Bean curd and mushrooms Peking style; Bean stuffed vine leaves; Borlotti scaloppini; Browned vegetable rice (in spiced yogurt sauce); Carrot, celery and butter bean lasagne; Cawl; Celery and almond casserole; Celery and peanut loaf; Cheesy ratatouille; Chick pea and Tahini casserole; Curried bean medley; Dahl Sag; Lentil cutlets; Lettuce in cucumber sauce; Multi-coloured stuffed peppers; Mushrooms à la Grecque; Mushrooms in garlic sauce; Nut paella; Pepper and onion stuffed crispy potatoes; Savoury Kasha; Soya bean casserole with crunchy topping; Spiced tofu; Spinach and red pepper gratinée; Spinach milles feuilles; Tacos Pueblo; Tofu pancakes with beansprouts; Tofu Satay; Vegetable curry.

DRESSED AND ACCOMPANYING DISHES

Bhindi in tamarind; Boules de pommes de terres; Brussels sprouts with chestnuts; Chinese-style beans; Courgettes nouvelles; Creamed chicory; Fresh asparagus with soured cream; Fried rice; Hot chilli runners; Hot cucumber in lemon verbena; Leek purée; Lyonnaise potatoes; Pilau rice; Poached fennel; Potatoes from Gujarat; Rosemary scented mushrooms; Spiced courgettes; Split peas in coconut milk; Stuffed potatoes; Swede and carrot purée; Tyrolean red cabbage; Vegetable platter.

PRESERVES AND SAUCES

Blackcurrant jam; Carrot marmalade; Marrow and ginger jam; Melba sauce; Redcurrant jelly; Soy and sherry sauce; Tomato and horseradish sauce; Vegan low-calorie sauce.

PUDDINGS, CAKES AND BREAD

Apple baskets; Baked apple cocktail; Baked jacket bananas with maple sauce; Chocolate and orange jelly cake; Early rhubarb crunch; Fruit crumble; Jamaica oranges; Malt fruit loaf; Non-dairy carob and pistachio pudding with apricot sauce; Raspberry jelly; Tipsy berries.

MENU SUGGESTIONS

'V' indicates suitable for vegans.

Mushroom soup
Spinach milles feuilles
Courgettes nouvelles
Insalata calda di vignola
Fresh fruit salad with thick yogurt

Artichoke soup
Devilled eggs
Boules de pommes de terre
Mange tout

Watercress soup
Chick pea and Tahini casserole
Savoury Kasha
Cauliflower florets
Tipsy berries

Lettuce soup
Brown vegetable rice in spiced yogurt sauce
Turban of cauliflower
Spinach salad
Marmalade fruit pudding with yogurt

Mulligatawny soup
Vegetable curry
Hot chilli runners
Lentil cutlets
Bhindi in tamarind
Brown rice
Budum dadh

V
Globe artichokes vinaigrette
Tofu pancakes with beansprouts
Celery and almond casserole
Lettuce in cucumber sauce
Tomato halves
Baked apple cocktail

Green lentil soup
Parsnips patties
Cheesy ratatouille
Roast buckwheat
Brussels sprouts
Raspberry jellies

Vichyssoise
Bean stuffed vine leaves
Brown rice
Hot slaw
Jamaica oranges

Little cheese and chervil pots
Soya bean casserole with crunchy
topping
Marrow rings
Broccoli
Pepper and onion stuffed crispy
potatoes
Stewed plums

Courgettes and pepper quiche
Mushroom and bean moussaka
Cucumber, tomato and watercress
salad
Apple baskets

Aubergine roast
Vegetable rice pilau
Swede and carrot purée
Lettuce and walnut salad
Chocolate orange jelly cake

Mushrooms in garlic sauce
Tofu Satay
Creamed sweetcorn and mung beans
Fried rice
Apple snow

V
Tomato salad
Spiced tofu
Vegetable curry
Brown rice
Tipsy berries

Beetroot soup
Asparagus mousse
Spinach salad
Planters salad
Sliced fresh tomatoes
Sliced cucumber
Wholemeal bread
Vegetarian cheese

V
Mushrooms à la Grecque
Spinach and red pepper gratinée
Bean stuffed vine leaves
Brussels sprouts with chestnuts
Baked jacket bananas

V
Carrot soup
Tofu pancakes with beansprouts
Leek purée
Savoury Kasha
Melon wedge

Barley soup
Borlotti scaloppini
Celery and peanut loaf
Praline ice cream

Dolmades
Bean curd and mushrooms Peking
style
Chinese-style beans
Spiced courgettes
Lyonnaise potatoes
Stewed apricots

V
Lettuce soup
Multi-coloured stuffed peppers
Vegetable platter
Vegan low-calorie sauce
Non-dairy carob and pistachio
pudding with apricot sauce

Carrot cocottes on marrow rings
Multi-coloured stuffed peppers
Lettuce and walnut salad
Tomato salad
Fudge bars

Artichoke salad
Curd cheese and pineapple potatoes
Tomatoes Florentine en croûte
Rosemary scented mushrooms
Fudge bars

V

Hot cucumber in lemon verbena
Carrot, celery and butter bean
lasagne
Kohlrabi salad
Beetroot salad
Green salad
Raspberry jelly

Deep-dish Spanish omelette
Potatoes from Gujarat
Split peas in coconut milk
Poached fennel
Chilled soufflé Grand Marnier

Cyprus salad
Almond apricotine stuffed pitta
Curried bean medley
Creamed chicory
Apple baskets

Eggs Benedict
Poached fennel
Mange tout
Cauliflower florets
Chocolate and carob roulade

Lettuce soup
Egg and bap lunch
Vegetable platter
Praline ice cream

Tomato and olive shir
Cawl
Steamed Bulgur
Nutmeat dumplings
Fresh fruit

Rosemary scented mushrooms
Tagliatelle verdi with soured cream
and chive sauce.
Tomato and Chinese leaf salad
Vegetarian cheese and wholemeal
biscuits.
Crisp fresh green dessert apples

Leek and tomato soup
Special rarebit en croûte
Cooked peas
Radish and lettuce salad
Basket of nuts

V

Celery and peanut loaf
Tyrolean red cabbage
Boiled potatoes
Baked apples

Selection of finger and fork food for 8-12 people:
Tacos peublo
Belporri puffs
Stuffed potatoes
Tomatoes Haloumi
Dahl Sag
Cheese and vegetable rarebit
Date and apple cake
Fudge bars
Carrot marmalade
Melon and ginger jam
Wholemeal bread

Fresh asparagus with soured cream
Nut paella
Leeks mimosa
Tomatoes Haloumi
Green salad
Chocolate dessert

Cawl
Nutmeat dumplings
Latkes
Early rhubarb crunch

Tomato vegetable ring
Walnut and aubergine gratin
Jacket potatoes
Sliced green beans
Chocolate carob roulade

Leek and tomato soup
Puffy omelettes with pimiento sauce
Jacket potatoes
Courgettes nouvelles
Walnut brownies

INDEX